Papua's Insecurity
State Failure in the
Indonesian Periphery

About the East-West Center

The East-West Center promotes better relations and understanding among the people and nations of the United States, Asia, and the Pacific through cooperative study, research, and dialogue. Established by the US Congress in 1960, the Center serves as a resource for information and analysis on critical issues of common concern, bringing people together to exchange views, build expertise, and develop policy options.

The Center's 21-acre Honolulu campus, adjacent to the University of Hawai'i at Mānoa, is located midway between Asia and the US mainland and features research, residential, and international conference facilities. The Center's Washington, DC, office focuses on preparing the United States for an era of growing Asia Pacific prominence.

The Center is an independent, public, nonprofit organization with funding from the US government, and additional support provided by private agencies, individuals, foundations, corporations, and governments in the region.

Policy Studies

an East-West Center series

Series Editors
Dieter Ernst and Marcus Mietzner

Description
Policy Studies presents original research on pressing economic and political policy challenges for governments and industry across Asia, and for the region's relations with the United States. Written for the policy and business communities, academics, journalists, and the informed public, the peer-reviewed publications in this series provide new policy insights and perspectives based on extensive fieldwork and rigorous scholarship.

Policy Studies is indexed in the *Web of Science Book Citation Index*. The *Web of Science* is the largest and most comprehensive citation index available.

Notes to Contributors
Submissions may take the form of a proposal or complete manuscript. For more information on the Policy Studies series, please contact the Series Editors.

Editors, Policy Studies
East-West Center
1601 East-West Road
Honolulu, Hawai'i 96848-1601
Tel: 808.944.7197
Publications@EastWestCenter.org
EastWestCenter.org/PolicyStudies

Policy
Studies | 73

Papua's Insecurity
State Failure in the
Indonesian Periphery

Bobby Anderson

Papua's Insecurity: State Failure in the Indonesian Periphery
Bobby Anderson

ISSN 1547-1349 (print) and 1547-1330 (electronic)
ISBN 978-0-86638-264-9 (print) and 978-0-86638-265-6 (electronic)

The views expressed are those of the author(s) and not necessarily those of the East-West Center.

Print copies are available from Amazon.com. Free electronic copies of most titles are available on the East-West Center website, at EastWestCenter.org/PolicyStudies, where submission guidelines can also be found. Questions about the series should be directed to:

Publications Office
East-West Center
1601 East-West Road
Honolulu, Hawai'i 96848-1601
Tel: 808.944.7145
Fax: 808.944.7376
EWCBooks@EastWestCenter.org
EastWestCenter.org/PolicyStudies

In Asia, print copies of all titles, and electronic copies of select Southeast Asia titles, co-published in Singapore, are available from:

Institute of Southeast Asian Studies
30 Heng Mui Keng Terrace
Pasir Panjang Road, Singapore 119614
publish@iseas.edu.sg
bookshop.iseas.edu.sg

Contents

List of Acronyms

ABC	Australian Broadcasting Corporation
AHRC	Asian Human Rights Commission
AI	Amnesty International
AusAID	Australian Agency for International Development
BAIS	Badan Intelijen Strategis, or military intelligence
BAPPENAS	Badan Perencanaan Pembangunan Nasional, or Indonesian State Development Planning Board
BIN	Badan Intelijen Negara, or domestic intelligence agency
BPS	Badan Pusat Statistik
BRR	Badan Rehabilitasi dan Rekonstruksi Wilayah dan Kehidupan Masyarakat Provinsi Nanggroe Aceh Darussalam Dan Kepulauan Nias Provinsi Sumatera Utara, or Agency of the Rehabilitation and Reconstruction for the Region and Community of Aceh and Nias
CPB	Communist Party of Burma
GAM	Gerakan Aceh Merdeka, or Free Aceh Movement

GDRP	gross domestic regional product
GIDI	Gereja Injili di Indonesia Papua, or Evangelical Church of Indonesia
HRW	Human Rights Watch
ICG	International Crisis Group
IPAC	Institute for Policy Analysis of Conflict
KINGMI	Kingmi Gospel Tabernacle Church of Papua
KIO	Kachin Independence Organization
KNPB	Komisi Nasional Papua Barat, or West Papua National Committee
KOMINDA	Komunitas Intelijen Daerah, or Regional Intelligence Communities
Kopassus	Komando Pasukan Khusus, or Special Forces Command
LIPI	Indonesian Institute of Sciences
OPM	Organisasi Papua Merdeka, or Free Papua Organization
OTK	Orang Tak Kenal, or unknown persons
PBI	Peace Brigades International
PEPERA	Penentuan Pendapat Rakyat, or Act of Free Choice
PNG	Papua New Guinea
PNPM	Program Nasional Pemberdayaan Masyarakat, or National Community Empowerment Program
PROSPEK	Program Strategis Pembangunan Kampung
RESPEK	Rencana Strategis Pembangunan Kampung
SATPOL PP	Satuan Polisi Pamong Praja, or Civil Service Police Unit

SNPK	Sistem Nasional Pemantauan Kekerasan, or National Violence Monitoring System
SSB	Single-SideBand modulation
SSR	security sector reform
TNI	Tentara Nasional Indonesia, or Indonesian armed forces
TPN	Tentara Pembebasan Nasional, or armed wing of the OPM
UN	United Nations
UP4B	Unit for Accelerated Development of Papua and West Papua
UWSP	United Wa State Party
ViCIS	Violent Conflict in Indonesia Study
VOC	Vereenigde Oost-Indische Compagnie, or Dutch East India Company

Executive Summary

Indonesia's easternmost provinces of Papua and Papua Barat, which are generally referred to as Papua, are the most violent and resource-rich areas of the country. Papua's absorption into Indonesia in an engineered "referendum" in 1969 remains openly contested by many Papuans and the international supporters of their cause. In Papua, Indonesian security actors battle the country's last active separatist insurgency. The vast majority of Indonesia's political prisoners are Papuans, while ordinary Papuans have the lowest incomes and the highest mortality in Indonesia. As a result, support for independence continues to be widespread.

But while military repression and indigenous resistance are major sources of violence in Papua, they are only one part of a complex topography of insecurity. As this study demonstrates, vigilantism, clan conflict, and other forms of horizontal violence produce more casualties than the vertical conflict that is often the exclusive focus of international accounts of the Papua problem. Similarly, Papua's coerced incorporation into Indonesia is not

Military repression and indigenous resistance are only part of a complex topography of insecurity in Papua

as unique as it is frequently made out to be; it mirrors a pattern of long-term annexation that also exists in other remote and highland areas of China, India, Indonesia, Myanmar, and Thailand. There, highland populations have found themselves on the receiving end of the violence of expanding lowland states. These annexed areas share similar histories of colonial settlement, land seizure, abuses by petty authorities, the rise of resistance, and violent state oppression.

Despite these similarities, however, this study highlights one major difference between Papua and other Asian remote and highland areas: no other area of highland South and Southeast Asia has experienced such an absence of the state and its services—except for territories in which debilitating insurgencies caused state services to collapse or never develop in the first place. In many indigenous areas of Papua, by contrast, the absence of the state is near-total, but there is no effective insurgency that caused this absence. Indeed, the Free Papua Organization is fragmented and miniscule. Rather than being the outcome of an all-encompassing rebellion, state failure in Papua is the consequence of a morass of policy dysfunction over time that serves to compound the insecurity that ordinary Papuans face.

No other area of highland Asia has experienced such an absence of the state and its services

While the Indonesian state has failed to deliver services to its ordinary citizens in Papua, it has co-opted the area's elites through the 2001 special autonomy law (*Otonomi Khusus,* or Otsus) and the process of administrative redistricting. To begin with, special autonomy has handed local elites a significant share of Papua's natural resource wealth. Designed to address political unrest and the challenges ordinary Papuans experience on a daily basis, special autonomy instead has provided income streams and no-show jobs to elites, while alleviating the central government of its responsibility to deliver the services that it failed to deliver in the first place. Meanwhile, the constant creation of new districts has allowed clans to carve out their own administrative structures to access government subsidies directly, further undermining already-weak rural health and education services. This elite co-optation has secured a fragile "peace" in Papua, but has done nothing to improve the living conditions of its citizens, especially in the poor highlands.

This study offers a new prism through which to view the complex host of difficulties troubling Papua. Illuminating the diverse and local sources of insecurity that point to a problem of too *little* state as opposed to too *much*, the following discussion challenges the notion that security issues in Papua are primarily related to the vertical conflict between the Indonesian state and the local armed insurgency. Rather, the picture of insecurity in Papua includes violence perpetuated by clans in constant conflict with one another; domestic violence and other nonpolitical clashes; chaotic and undisciplined state security actors operating in an outdated and inefficient hierarchical structure; and separatist groups that act more like local gangs than like a rebel army. Papua's insecurity is significantly aggravated by uncontrolled migration, an absence of the rule of law, failing health and education services, and extreme levels of corruption. Consequently, this study concludes with policy suggestions to improve conditions for indigenous Papuans, of which the most important is the urgent need for the creation of a coordinating ministry for Papua overseeing the equally urgent provincial centralization of government services. Further, the Indonesian state needs to take fresh steps toward achieving reconciliation; reforming a security sector steeped in a culture of violence and impunity; enacting controls on migration and administrative redistricting; and developing a new indigenous-centered development policy.

Papua's Insecurity
State Failure in the
Indonesian Periphery

Introduction

Much has been written about violent conflict in Indonesia's eastern-most provinces, Papua and Papua Barat (hereafter collectively referred to as Papua). Despite the large amount of literature, however, most works on the subject have featured one common analytical theme: that is, insecurity in Papua is regarded predominantly as an issue of indigenous people threatened by the state (Brundige et al. 2004, Elmslie 2003, Elmslie and Webb-Gannon 2013, King 2004, King 2006, Monbiot 1989, TAPOL 1988, Wing and King 2005). But while military repression and indigenous resistance are major factors conditioning contemporary insecurity in the region, they are only a small part of the story. Rather, vigilantism, clan conflict, and other forms of horizontal violence are leading to more casualties than the vertical conflict that is assumed to be the main conflict there.

This diversity of conflict patterns also questions traditional inter-pretations of the role of the state in Papua. Whereas the Indonesian state is often viewed as a repressive and omnipotent actor in Papua, in reality, many areas in the region are marked by the *absence* of the state rather than its dominance. This is particularly true in the high-lands, which form the epicenter of violent conflict in Papua. Unlike in other conflict-prone regions of Southeast Asia, where the absence of the state is (or was) the result of large-scale insurgencies, the weakness of the state in highland Papua has other sources. For instance, the absence of the "Bamar" state in those parts of Kachin Myanmar controlled by the Kachin Independence Organization, and the collapse of state services in Aceh's eastern separatist "heartlands" at the height of the 1976–2005 conflict between the government of Indonesia and the Free Aceh Movement (*Gerakan Aceh Merdeka,* or GAM), were to be expected, given the extensive fighting between rebels and the state. In Papua, however, a miniscule and fragmented insurgency, the Free Papua Organization (*Organisasi Papua Merdeka,* or OPM) is only active in a few subdistricts. But outside of select towns, the absence of the state is near-total in Papua's highlands. This failure is not the intentional result of government policy. It is, as this paper argues, the result of a morass of policy failures over time, aggravated by limitations to state capacity and competence.

While Papua's conflict patterns are products of its specific historical development, and many authors have highlighted the uniqueness of the Papuan case, its coerced incorporation into the Indonesian state is comparable to the experiences of other populations in remote and highland areas of South and Southeast Asia, where "the friction of terrain" limited the effective reach of empires (Scott 2009, 43). There, minority groups existing in state-resistant social structures have found themselves on the receiving end of the violence of expanding lowland states. These highlanders in China, India, Indonesia, Myanmar, and Thailand share similar histories of colonial settlement and land seizure, agricultural and labor conversion, imposition of taxes and rent-seeking by petty authorities, the rise of resistance, and resulting state oppression of an often brutal nature. Thus, any discussion of the highland and remote lowland Papua experience needs to contextualize it within the framework of the conflict structures found in other remote highland communities, in Southeast Asia and beyond (Scott 2009).

Since the end of Indonesia's authoritarian New Order regime in 1998, Papua has undergone significant change. While New Order Papua's relative stability was due to the brutal responses of state security actors toward the slightest hint of insurrection, contemporary Papua's relative calm is due to the co-opting of Papuan elites through the law known as special autonomy (*Otonomi Khusus,* or Otsus), which along with decentralization transferred the responsibility for health, education, and other services to the subnational level. Special autonomy has provided income streams and sinecures to indigenous elites, while alleviating the central government of its responsibility to deliver services—which it had failed to deliver in the first place. In the highlands especially, administrative fragmentation (*pemekaran*) has served as a tool of co-option that allows clans to create their own districts and subdistricts; subsequently, these clans have increased their national administrative subsidies through fictitious population increases. Special autonomy and administrative fragmentation, however, are not only mediums by which the state co-opts Papuans; they are also the means by which Papuans co-opt the state. Indonesian influence in the highlands is both vast and shallow—in the remotest areas, it is only apparent in the tattered uniforms of illiterate civil servants who don't speak Bahasa Indonesia, the national language.[1] Behind this veneer of state co-optation, an older Melanesian system of conflict and exchange persists that favors kinship and redistribution. Provision of services to a constituency in this system is not a priority, and health and education budgets are absorbed by the traditional system of exchange. Horizontal conflict between these clans, as argued here, is leading to more Papuan casualties than vertical state-society or separatist conflict.

> *Special autonomy and administrative fragmentation allow the state to co-opt Papuans, and Papuans to co-opt the state*

This study, which is based on more than five years of research and work in rural and highland Papua, interprets the phenomenon of violence in the area within the context of other remote highland territories in Asia; shows that commonplace notions of insecurity in Papua as primarily being caused by state oppression are missing other important dimensions of the conflict; and argues that these simplifications impede solutions to Papua's quagmire of political and development issues. In doing so, this study offers a more nuanced prism through which to view Papua: that is, as the subject of an ongoing and incompetently executed annexation that is only recently emerging, in the last two decades, from an undifferentiated early stage concentrated solely on coercion and exploitation. Importantly, Papua's experience is similar not only to many Asian highlands and peripheries, but also to other areas of Indonesia; it serves as a bellwether for the progress of governance reform across Indonesia. Special autonomy has allowed the threadbare presence of the national-level government to recede from nearly every sector that could theoretically provide benefit to rural and indigenous citizens. Only the security sector remains, and it has shown a surprising tolerance for anarchy and violence in Papua, so long as it is not directed at the state.

The arguments are developed in four sections. The first section demonstrates the commonalities Papua shares with other remote and highland areas in Asia, and discusses Papua's incorporation into the Netherlands East Indies, and later into Indonesia. It does so by applying the frameworks developed by James C. Scott and Joel S. Migdal, and shows that Papua's incorporation differs from the experiences of many other parts of the Indonesian archipelago because of its rugged topography and the resilience of its egalitarian social structures, especially in the highlands. The second section demonstrates the diverse and local sources of insecurity that often illustrate the impact of having too little state, as opposed to too much. Section three contrasts the area's multifaceted insecurity with the widespread assertion that Papua is in the grip of a tightly controlled police state. The conclusion, finally, offers policy suggestions to improve conditions for indigenous Papuans. These recommendations include the reform of a largely unaccountable local security sector, the centralization of health and education services, a new and enforceable migration policy, and a moratorium on redistricting.

> *Special autonomy allows the threadbare presence of the national-level government to recede from nearly every sector*

Papua and Its Highlands: Colonization and Annexation

The recent experiences of highland Papua's Dani, Lani, Mee, Mek, Nduga, Yali, and other tribes bear some resemblance to the past experiences of the archipelago's Dayaks, Gayo, and Tengger highlanders; Myanmar's Chin, Kachin, Karen, Karenni, Shan, and Wa; Southwest China's Akha, Lahu, Miao, Yao, and Yi; and Northeast India's Assamese, Kuki, Meitei, and Naga. For many centuries, these peoples have all resisted the colonial depredations of lowland states. They dwell, often purposefully, in state-resistant spaces. They cultivate staple crops that are hard to seize and tax, and their food sources and cultivation methods allow for wide population disbursement, as opposed to the population concentrations required for rice production. They live in rugged topographies, and political entities are fractious and impermanent due to an egalitarianism that resists strong local rulers. Their religions, new or adopted, mark them as different from nearby "lowland" states that have sought to absorb them. With the exception of the Gayo and the Tengger highlanders, the majority of these populations are Baptist Christians. For them, the story of the Israelites finds particular resonance in its themes of persecution, exile, and redemption of a chosen people. The Papuan concept of *Merdeka,* or freedom, as the cure for all ills is pregnant with such millenarian imagery. Prophets constantly appear in these populations. Melanesian cargo cultism also has a similar theme: a restoration of goods taken away by outsiders.[2]

These commonalities made highlanders more historically resistant to state oppression than other groups (Scott 2009). The differences between these highlanders can be found in the timing of their incorporation into larger states and the success or failure of that incorporation. The more recent the incorporation and the less benefit received from the state, the less abstract the idea of secession. Highland Papua and Kachin are in the midst of an incorporation process that Sichuan and Yunnan finished generations ago. And Arunachal Pradesh, Assam, Chin, Kachin, Nagaland, Shan, and Papua—all of which have more recent histories of annexation—still host armed insurgencies. It is within this context that the history of Papua's integration into the Indonesian state needs to be embedded.

A Brief History of Papua in Indonesia

Papua and Papua Barat are Indonesia's easternmost provinces. Home to 3.6 million people (Badan Pusat Statistik 2010), Papua is a largely undeveloped, sparsely populated area the size of California. It is 90 percent forested and rich in natural resources, ranging from fisheries to coal, copper, and gold. To simply say that Papua has a rugged topography does not give the land its due. Papua's interior remained impenetrable to outsiders for much of Dutch colonial rule, with the exception of occasional incursions to inland swamps like the southern coast, where the Netherlands East Indies' political prisoners were exiled after the failed communist uprisings on Java in 1926. Papua's

The majority of indigenous Papuans live in the underdeveloped highlands

coast is distinguished by swamps and alluvial plains that give way to the foothills of a mountain range that bisects the territory and essentially cuts off the north from the south in the same way that the Hindu Kush leaves Afghanistan as two distinct entities. The highlands are not simply a geographic line in this bisection; they form the interior in its entirety, with several peaks reaching higher than 4,000 meters. The majority of indigenous inhabitants of Papua live in the economically most underdeveloped highlands, setting them apart from the better-educated and generally more affluent coastal and lowland Papuans.

In the heart of the Papuan highlands lies the Baliem Valley, a hub of overlapping highland Melanesian cultures of war and exchange that did not experience contact with outsiders until 1938. A mosaic of smaller settlements was concealed within the folds of the massifs surrounding the Baliem Valley, giving home to a mass of clans and extended families. These clans were often at war with one another, creating a human landscape just as volatile and subject to erosion and tension as the mountains themselves. This volatility continues to the present: Papua's fragmentation along tribal and clan lines has resulted in 312 officially designated tribes, thousands of clans, and a minimum of 269 indigenous languages (Marshall and Beehler 2007, 108). The area is one of the most linguistically diverse in the world.

The power of traditional Melanesian leaders rests upon redistribution of wealth to followers and supporters, and is always in flux (Sahlins 1963). Internal conflicts over leadership result in the constant formation of new clans, which are the primary markers of identity in the region. These contentious collective relationships, and a history of both constant war between clans and shifting and unpredictable allegiances within clans, has led to small, isolated populations spread across rugged topography, and settled in defensible areas that are distant from other settlements. The intensity of clan wars has lessened over time, but the isolation of the various clan-based communities in the highlands remains a dominant feature of Papuan society.

These extremes—in topography, in ethnic diversity, in contention and egalitarianism—link rural Papua, and highland Papua in particular, to other areas of the Southeast Asian highland massif, which is sometimes called Zomia (Van Schendel 2002). However, the fundamental difference between these areas relates to their accessibility. Nagaland, Kachin, and other highland Southeast Asian areas lie on one of the world's greatest migratory routes, and James C. Scott (Scott 2009) and others postulate that these areas accepted wave after wave of migrants fleeing their respective homes during different eras of lowland state incorporation. In highland Papua, on the other hand, there were no such known migration waves, although the number of languages and identities is just as diverse in Papua as in highland Southeast Asia. The main reason for the absence of intra-Papuan migration flows into the highlands was the peripheral nature of Papua's coastal and lowland areas to the expanding Netherlands East Indies economy. Consequently, there was little oppression that could have caused inhabitants of the lowlands to flee to the less-governed highland interior.

Papua's development was embedded in broader patterns of Indonesia's colonization. In the 17th and 18th centuries, the Dutch East India Company (*Vereenigde Oost-Indische Compagnie,* or VOC) violently colonized pre-existing lowland kingdoms, whose cultural and tax infrastructure was generally based on rice cultivation and maritime trade. As the VOC expanded its sphere of influence to the peripheries of these earlier kingdoms (ironically, often former colonizers themselves), it encountered sparser populations subsisting on fishing or limited trade. Like the empires it now replaced, the VOC established suzerainty over all economic activity in the conquered territories. Successful traders who did not submit to its writ, such as the nutmeg-producing Banda Islanders, were killed or deported and enslaved, with a more pliant population settling in their place. As the VOC consolidated its territory and, after 1800, morphed into the Dutch colonial state, the approach to governance became less ruthless. Pirates gave way to administrators, and indigenous proxies emerged, with the "Chinese" (Taylor 2003, 129) collecting taxes, and a class of petty appointees—often drawn from a pre-existing indigenous population of aristocratic *priyayi* elites—lorded over administrative parcels.

Papua, however, lacked good soil and concentrated populations; it had little to trade beyond feathers from birds of paradise and similar artificially valued bric-a-brac. Papua did not generate revenues high enough to justify colonization by the VOC, nor did the miniscule population constitute a market for goods. The British had comparable experiences as they expanded into the highlands of Northeast India and later Myanmar (Kumar Das 2007; Leach 1954; Rajagopalan 2008; Scott 2009; Smith 1994). Since the economic justification for their oppressive presence was lacking, the colonizers were happy to appoint pre-existing rulers to govern "on their behalf," thus allowing them to concentrate on the lowland areas that served as both tax base and market for their manufactured goods. Like the East India Companies of both the English and the Dutch, highly organized religious institutions served as important proxy actors for state expansion, converting susceptible populations, preaching subservience, providing occasional health and education services, and registering births, deaths, and marriages. To a lesser and differentiated but still notable extent, the American, Dutch, English, and other denominations that arrived in the post-colonial era provided the same services, as do indigenous Papuan churches, such as the Evangelical Church of Indonesia (*Gereja Injili di Indonesia Papua*, or GIDI) and the Kingmi Gospel Tabernacle Church of Papua (*Gereja Kemah Injil Papua,* or GKIP/KINGMI).

In western Papua, the pro-Dutch Sultan of Tidore in the islands of North Maluku claimed sovereignty, and while the Dutch initially recognized this claim (McGibbon 2004, 6), the colonial power began direct rule in the late 1800s. The Dutch presence was limited to a few islands (Yapen, Biak) and coastal towns, however. The rest of the area was left to its own devices (Rutherford 2003, 182). In areas where Dutch authorities and their Malukan administrative proxies settled, mostly along the coasts, their presence gave rise to indigenous elites who continue to dominate Papua's civil service structures today. Christian missionaries first arrived in Manokwari during this same time frame. Protestant Christianity rapidly spread among Papuans,[3] which made them a favored population by the Dutch, though not as much as

> *Indigenous elites in coastal areas continue to dominate Papua's civil service structures today*

the politically and economically better positioned Ambonese, Mina-hasans, and Timorese.

Papuans and other peripheral populations were absent from Indo-nesian nationalist movements, which were populated by indigenous elites in lowland areas central to the colonial economy—Java and Su-matra especially. In India, Myanmar, and Vietnam, highlanders were absent from lowland anti-colonial nationalist movements because they were inimical to highland interests (Scott 2009). Unlike Papua, these highlanders experienced colonization by the same lowland states that were struggling against their own foreign colonization, and the cur-rent colonizers were allies with the highlanders against their former oppressors. The remoteness of highland Papua left it with no such ex-perience. The relationship between the Dutch and nearly all Papuans was marked—beyond the common bond of religion—by the relative absence of foreign colonial power. The typical chronological sequence of highland Southeast Asia—first, lowland empires were formed, then highlands were colonized, and finally western colonization dominated lowland empires (Scott 2009)—was reversed in Papua, with the low-land's colonization of the highlands occurring as the final phase.

Throughout the decolonization era after 1945, the Assamese, Kachin, Karen, Montagnards, Wa, and others sought to distance themselves from their post-colonial states during or immediately af-ter independence. These highland groups sought their own indepen-dence through appeals to waning colonial powers, but their claims were not recognized; the borders stood. Select highland populations moved to defend their interests, leading to their violent recolonization by the recently decolonized. But the Dutch refused to include Papua in their negotiations with the new Indonesian republic (Bone 1958). Numerous post-1945 Dutch governments tenaciously adhered to this position, eventually finding justifications for such intransigence in a paternalistic regard for the welfare of Papuans that did not previously exist. The importance of Papua in the Indonesian nationalist psyche grew as a counterpoint: Papua became one last battle in an incomplete revolution. The Papuans themselves were peripheral in this high-level political game (van der Kroef 1968).

While the Dutch position was born from vindictiveness, in 1949 the colonial power began a new indigenous education policy in order to create a cadre of indigenous administrators who would govern an independent Papua. By the end of the 1950s, Papuans had already been placed in senior administrative positions (Visser 2013). The Dutch built an educational system and established a semi-legislative body, the *Nieuw Guinea Raad*. Nascent and diverse articulations of Papuan nationalism began to mature at this time (Chauvel 2005a and 2005b), and many themes of the current independence movement have roots in arguments originally articulated by the Dutch (Chauvel 2005a and 2005b; Bone 1958). Between the end of World War II and the colonial power's departure in 1962, the Dutch empowered Papuans in a way that the Indonesians never would in the half century that followed.

During the Cold War, the Kennedy administration, in order to defuse one of the Indonesian Communist Party's most popular causes and prevent Indonesia from drifting into the communist "orbit," brokered the 1962 New York Agreement between the Netherlands and Indonesia. The agreement allowed for a period of United Nations (UN) trusteeship under an Indonesian administration in Papua, followed by a referendum (Drooglever 2010, Saltford 2000). The Indonesian soldiers who entered Papua in 1963 immediately went on a looting spree (Wanandi 2012). The expansionist violence, bureaucratic pettiness, and marginalization that Papua avoided under the Dutch had at last arrived. Educated Papuans began to leave. In 1969, President Suharto[4] dispatched his intelligence operator Ali Murtopo to manipulate the Act of Free Choice (*Penentuan Pendapat Rakyat,* or PEPERA). In lieu of "one man, one vote," roughly 1,020 pliable local leaders voted, on behalf of their assumed constituencies, for integration into Indonesia (Drooglever 2010, May 1978, Saltford 2000, Simpson 2010, Wanandi 2012). While this occurred in a pervasive environment of intimidation and fear (May 1978, *Herald Sun* 2011, van der Kroef 1968), the vote was nevertheless recognized by the UN and the United States.

In response to the Indonesian expansion, Seth Rumkorem and Jacob Prai founded the Free Papua Organization (OPM) in 1965 (Bell et al. 1986, Chauvel 2005a, Osborne 1985, Premdas 1985). OPM's founders soon split with one another, and by the 1970s OPM functioned not as a hierarchically organized paramilitary structure but as an idea, with self-identifying armed groups operating under its umbrella. Throughout the 1970s and 1980s, occasional clashes occurred. The most significant OPM action was its role in the 1977–78 Dani uprising (AHRC 2013), and a much smaller 1984 uprising in Jayapura that led to roughly 10,000 Papuans fleeing to Papua New Guinea (PNG) after the army's violent countermeasures (Osborne 1985, Bell et al. 1986).

After PEPERA, Indonesia "developed" Papua through non-Papuan administrators, who were mostly active-duty Indonesian military. Development prioritized internal and external security, followed by resource extraction. The Papuan civil servants trained by the Dutch were not trusted by Indonesia, and many left the country. Papuan experience with Indonesians from other areas of the archipelago grew as interisland migration increased; in fact, transmigration programs begun under the Dutch reached their zenith in the New Order. The programs effectively engineered demographic change, and the preponderance of transmigration settlements along the PNG border served national security functions.[5] State bureaucracy outside select towns, on the other hand, remained piecemeal and ineffective. In rural areas, church structures inherited from the Dutch era provided health and education services to a minority of the population until the 1990s. This system was gradually supplanted by an encroaching

The only interaction many Papuans have with the state is through local Indonesian armed forces or police

and incompetent state that sought to take over such services, but often destroyed them instead (Anderson 2013a, 2013b, 2014a, 2014c). A shallow imposition of bureaucracy occurred in some areas, with officials appointed and uniformed, from the village head on upwards. But these appointees had no observable duties. Many areas remained so impenetrable that even civil servant uniforms were not to be found. Thus, many Papuans have had little interaction with the non-coercive state; their only interaction has often been with local Indonesian armed forces (*Tentara Nasional Indonesia*, or TNI) or police.

Typically, lowland security actors posted to highland areas develop parasitic relations with host communities. For instance, Myanmar's army, the *Tatmadaw*, has traditionally exhibited a violence toward their hosts that the TNI has only displayed in discrete "pacification" campaigns—such as the one in Mapenduma in 1996, and on a larger scale in the Baliem Valley in 1977–78. Otherwise, the TNI treated

Papuans in the same manner they did Indonesians suspected of disloyalty toward the state in other parts of the archipelago—that is, callously and exploitatively, and sometimes brutally. Eyewitness accounts of massacres and aerial attacks from this period (AHRC 2013, Osborne 1985) illustrated the indiscriminate violence of the state toward its own citizens, and an inability to distinguish between combatant and civilian. However, one important aspect of the history of state violence against Papua's highlanders has often gone unrecognized. While some clans fell victim to TNI's depredations, others benefitted from, and actively assisted in, the destruction of their clan enemies. Those who have testified to the violence of the TNI also frequently testified to the "others" who joined in the attacks. Indonesia's incorporation of the highlands in the 1970s and 1980s is full of such instances of cooperation. Importantly, clan wars continued throughout this period, albeit with TNI acting as a force multiplier for the clans that aligned with them first.[6]

> *In the 70s and 80s, the TNI acted as a force multiplier for clans that aligned with it*

The end of the New Order in 1998 was marked by a resurgence of Papuan independence aspirations and violent crackdowns by security forces, the most famous of which was the Biak massacre.[7] This period is well documented elsewhere (Chauvel and Bhakti 2004, Chauvel 2005b, ICG 2003–12, Timmer 2007a and 2007b), but a brief summary is necessary here. In early 1999, B.J. Habibie allowed a referendum on independence in East Timor (Cribb 2001), and many Papuans consequently demanded the same. It was not to be. However, the brief period of openness under Habibie's successor Abdurrahman Wahid (1999–2001), which became known as the Papuan Spring, resulted in the temporary decriminalization of Papuan nationalist symbols, such as the *Bintang Kejora* (morning star); the deepening of dialogue with Jakarta; and the establishment of special autonomy. As an implicit alternate to a referendum, special autonomy returned the majority of revenues from Papua's mineral wealth to the province, to be used for health, education, and other development needs. Affirmative action policies in special autonomy would eventually place Papuans in the majority of leadership and civil servant positions. The Papuan People's Council (*Majelis Rakyat Papua,* or MRP) was created to safeguard

Papuan cultures, although it took until 2006 before a weakened version of this body was inaugurated (Kivimaki and Thorning 2002, McGibbon 2004, Mietzner 2009, Timmer 2007b).

Arguably, the dialogue of that era may have eventually led to reconciliation in the form of a commonly accepted history and an acknowledgement of state abuses. Instead, the Papuan Spring ended with Wahid's impeachment in July 2001 and his successor, Megawati Sukarnoputri, taking a hardline approach to anything resembling "separatism." Special autonomy was emasculated, and in direct contravention to that law, Megawati divided Papua into Papua proper and Papua Barat. A third province was attempted, but deadly riots in Timika stayed the government's hand (ICG 2003). The use of separatist symbols was re-criminalized, punishable by charges of rebellion, with dozens jailed for such offenses since Megawati's presidency.[8] Dialogue ended. It cannot be emphasized enough how the actions of the Megawati government destroyed the modicum of trust that Wahid had built. Much of Papua's political volatility, and the lack of faith in the word of "Jakarta," directly stems from her decisions, and those of the shapers of her policies, among them the intelligence chief, Hendropriyono, and the army chief, Ryamizard Ryacudu.[9] Ironically, after having been sidelined by Yudhoyono between 2004 and 2014, both now serve again in the current administration of Joko Widodo, with Hendropriyono as an informal security advisor and Ryacudu as defense minister. As for the aspects of special autonomy that were to be implemented by the province, the law was enacted without clear guidelines for implementation and ultimately degenerated into a slush fund (Anderson 2013a, 2013b, 2014a, 2014b, 2014c).

Contemporary Papua

Despite the political upheaval affecting Papua since the 1960s, its social reality has been stagnant for decades. Outside of the cities and towns, much of rural Papua remains developmentally largely unchanged from the time of the Dutch. Transportation infrastructure has barely improved outside of air services. Communications infrastructure is frustratingly weak, with much communication in the highlands occurring via SSB radio that expanded with missionary air transport networks. Access to health and education is extremely limited, and the few existing services accessible to rural Papuans have deteriorated.

Nowhere is this chronic state of neglect over the course of Indonesian rule more apparent than in revisiting the forgotten documents produced by the Fund of the United Nations for the Development of West Irian (FUNDWI): *Report on Agricultural Production in West Irian* (1967) and, in particular, *A Design for Development in West Irian* (1968). The development issues of today's Papua—including transport, health, education, livelihoods, and affirmative action—were first cited in these publications. Indeed, the reports from the 1960s read like a description of Papua's contemporary social problems.

Indigenous Papuans measure low in human development and other indicators vis-à-vis both the Indonesian provinces and Papua's migrant populations. Most Papuans live in rural areas, and rural poverty rates there are the highest in Indonesia: in Papua province, 40.72 percent of the population live below the official poverty line, and in Papua Barat, this rate is 36.89 percent. The poverty rate of Indonesia's third-worst performing province, Maluku, stands at only 26.3 percent. Comparing rural and urban populations is telling, as urban areas host the migrant and civil servant population: the urban poverty rate in Papua province is 5.22 percent, while it is 4.89 percent in Papua Barat. This is better than the national urban poverty average, which stands at 8.52 percent (BPS 2013). Of course, this means that rural poverty in both provinces, among indigenous and particularly highland populations, is disproportionally worse.

The situation in the area of education is equally dire. Papuans have the highest rates of illiteracy in Indonesia. In fact, the illiteracy rate for children under 15 *increased* from 25.54 percent in 2003 to 34.31 percent in 2012 (the national average is 6.75 percent). But given the widespread illiteracy in the highlands of Papua province (Anderson 2013b), even these figures may be too low. On the other hand, Papua Barat's under-15 illiteracy rate reflects that province's more advanced development: from a 2006 rate of 11.45 percent (the first year illiteracy figures were measured in the new province), the number has declined to 5.26 percent in 2012, which is better than the national average (BPS 2013). Papua province's 2010–2011 provincial development plan for basic and secondary education

> *The illiteracy rate for children under 15 actually increased from 2003 to 2012*

indicated that school enrollment for children aged between seven and twelve throughout the province is 73 percent. In other words, at least 100,000 out of the 400,000 children in the province are not in school. Junior secondary enrollment is 55 percent and senior secondary just 37 percent (Dinas Pendidikan Propinsi Papua 2011).

Similarly, indigenous Papuans have the lowest life expectancy, and the highest infant, child, and maternal mortality rates in Indonesia. The 2012 *Indonesia Demographic and Health Survey Preliminary Report* prepared by Badan Pusat Statistik, the Ministry of Health, the National Population and Family Planning Board, and other agencies indicate that in Papua province only 40 percent of babies were delivered by a skilled provider; in Jakarta, the rate was 99 percent. In Papua province, 27 percent of babies were delivered in a health facility; in Jakarta, the rate was 96 percent. In Jakarta, 22 babies out of 1,000 died in the period covered by the report, but in Papua province this number was 54 and in Papua Barat it was 74. In Jakarta, 31 out of 1,000 children under the age of five died, but in Papua Barat this number was 109 and in Papua province it was 115 (BPS 2012). Death rates tend to worsen in the remote areas for which statistics are available. The French NGO Médecins du Monde, which worked in Puncak Jaya for a number of years, estimated in 2008 that the infant mortality rate in the district stood at 85–150 per 1,000 live births (Rees et al. 2008, 641).

Papua already has the lowest basic child vaccination rates in Indonesia: 74.3 percent in Papua province and 72.7 percent in Papua Barat. But these rates are for both migrant and indigenous children. Health workers estimate that less than 50 percent of indigenous Papuan children receive them.[10] In the highlands, the majority of children do not.[11] In many new districts, no vaccinations have occurred since the split from the old district. For instance, immunizations ended in the new district of Yahukimo in 2002 within months of the district's formation, a result of the cold storage vaccination chain breaking down. Papuans have the highest tuberculosis infection rates in the country. Health foundations estimate a minimum 10 percent infection rate in Wamena town. In the rest of the highlands, it may be higher still. Papuans also have the highest HIV/AIDS rates in Indonesia, and one of the fastest-growing HIV infection rates in Asia. In 2006, the Australian development agency AusAID predicted that by 2025, while Indonesia would have a nationwide infection rate of 1.08 percent, HIV rates in Papua would rise to 7 percent (AusAID 2006, 101). However, health care workers in Wamena already estimate a prevalence of at least 10 percent in their region.[12] HIV rates in remote areas of the highlands are unknown, but the number of young men, women, and children dying of unknown causes is higher than the already abysmal provincial averages. A link to the spread of HIV is likely.

The employment patterns in Papua underscore the territory's lack of socioeconomic modernization. Papua's indigenous populations are generally employed in subsistence agricultural practices, while a growing number of elites are dependent upon the state for employment (Anderson 2014c). This is a commonality that connects Papua to other peripheral areas of Indonesia, and to other highland territories such as Northeast India.

Insecurity in Contemporary Papua

Much of the literature on contemporary Papua has focused on its seemingly interminable security problems, especially the continued separatist violence. But security patterns in Papua are not uniform. The very expression "Papua conflict" implies a singularity: one fight involving two parties. However, this is a highly problematic proposition. Security conditions and threats change as one crosses innumerable administrative, church, clan (*suku*), extended family (*marga*), and linguistic boundaries. These borders subdivide the entire region into an impermeable multiplicity of often overlapping territories dominated by different actors, some of them coercive and rent-seeking. Nowhere is this truer than in the highlands, with their linguistic and social diversity that accompanies low population densities in mountainous terrain.

Security conditions change as one crosses administrative, church, clan, extended family, and linguistic boundaries

An important element of the diversity of Papua's security landscape is the stability found in much of the area. Most of Papua Barat and southern Papua, and portions of the highlands (Enarotali, Wamena/Baliem) have long been incorporated and commoditized, with highland treks marketed to foreigners. In Fakfak, Kaimana, Sorong,

Notes: This map is the author's attempt to show the nuances of Papua's insecurity and is by no means comprehensive.

"Land/resource conflict" reflects conflict between Papuans and large-scale natural resource extraction operations. It does not indicate more common small-scale natural resource conflicts between local actors.

Red dots signify areas of recurrent violence, not every violent incident.

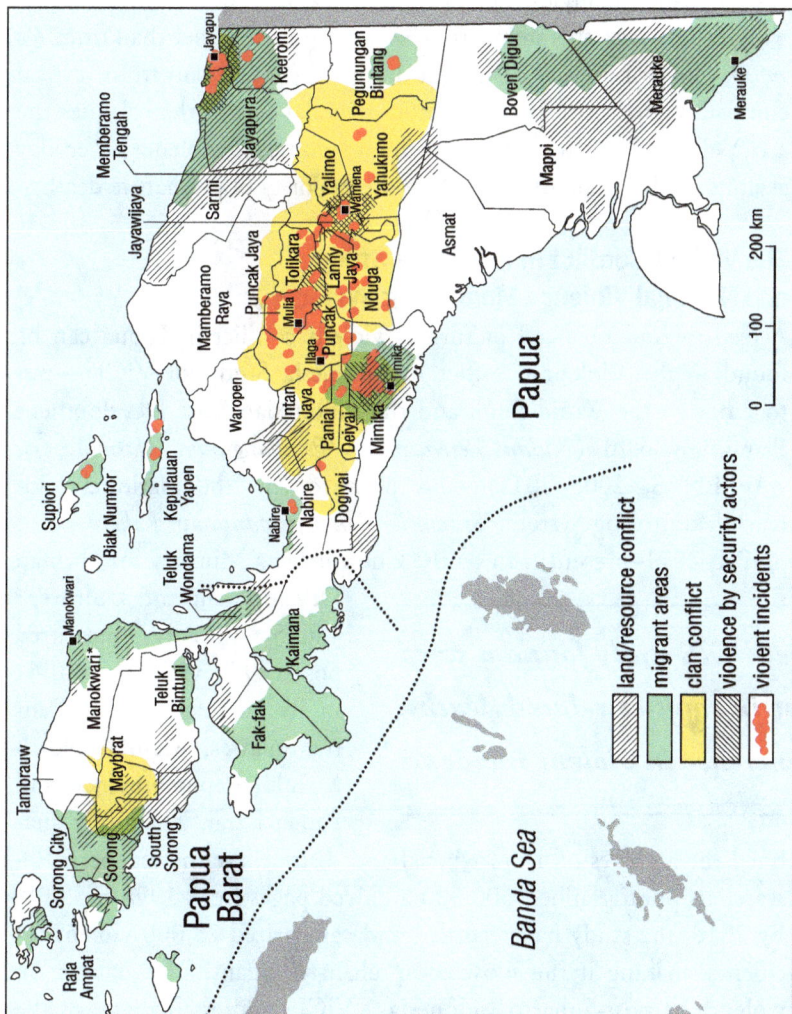

Papua Barat

Raja Ampat
Sorong City
Tambrauw
Sorong
South Sorong
Maybrat
Manokwari *
Teluk Bintuni
Fak-fak
Kaimana
Teluk Wondama
Biak Numfor
Kepulauan Yapen
Supiori
Nabire
Nabire
Dogiyai
Deiyai
Paniai
Intan Jaya
Waropen
Mamberamo Raya
Puncak Jaya
Mulia
Tolikara
Puncak
Lanny Jaya
Jaya
Nduga
Mimika
Mimika
Ilaga
Sarmi
Jayawijaya
Mamberamo Tengah
Yalimo
Wamena
Yalukimo
Pegunungan Bintang
Jayapura
Jayapura
Keerom
Jayapu
Asmat
Boven Digul
Mappi
Merauke
Merauke

Papua

Banda Sea

land/resource conflict
migrant areas
clan conflict
violence by security actors
violent incidents

0   100   200 km

Yapen, Biak, Merauke, Nabire, and other areas, a small-town banality exists. Jayapura has its own shopping mall; another has finally been completed in Wamena after years of intermittent construction due to the high price of cement. Only a few areas of active vertical-separatist contestation in the highlands remain. Nevertheless, Papua's multifaceted issues are often reduced to security actions against indigenous persons alleged to constitute genocide (Brundige et al. 2004; Elmslie 2003; Elmslie and Webb-Gannon 2013; King 2004; King 2006; Wing and King 2005)—an image shakily built upon the real past savagery of state security actors. Presently, however, the state is one element of many in Papua's insecurity, and as the following section will demonstrate, this stems from *not enough* state rather than from *too much*. Only a minority of violent deaths in Papua result from vertical conflict. Vigilantism, the ubiquitous popular justice that plagues the archipelago, along with an epidemic of domestic violence, everyday assaults, and clan fights, constitute the majority of premature deaths.

The Violent Conflict in Indonesia Study and National Violence Monitoring System

A realistic and nuanced picture of violent conflict in Papua can be found in the Violent Conflict in Indonesia Study, or ViCIS—put together by the World Bank and the Indonesian State Development Planning Board (*Badan Perencanaan Pembangunan Nasional,* or BAPPENAS, 2008–2011)—and its successor, the National Violence Monitoring System (*Sistem Nasional Pemantauan Kekerasan,* or SNPK, 2011–present) run by the Coordinating Ministry for Human Development and Culture.[13] ViCIS initially measured post-1998 violent conflict in six provinces: Aceh, Central Sulawesi, Maluku, North Maluku, Papua province, and Papua Barat. The study analyzed the archives of 46 provincial and district-level newspapers. Researchers photographed 600,000 archived pages from 1998 to 2008. By 2010, the study had recorded and categorized 28,000 violent incidents, making it the most comprehensive quantitative dataset on violence in post-Suharto Indonesia.[14] ViCIS addressed many of the

The ViCIS study found a steep decline in conflict-related deaths, but an increase in violent incidents

flaws found within the United Nations Support Facility for Indonesian Recovery (UNSFIR) conflict database (1990–2003), which only recorded intergroup conflicts. Among others, the ViCIS recorded every violent incident reported. The study found a steep decline in conflict-related *deaths,* from a peak of 3,500 per year in 1999, but also discovered an increase in violent *incidents* in all areas except for Aceh. The biggest climb in overall violence occurred in Maluku.

Using the years 2004 to 2008 as a representative sample, ViCIS found that, when adjusted for population size, the provinces of Papua and Papua Barat suffered the highest number of violent deaths in Indonesia. A total of 6,552 violent incidents in that period resulted in 596 deaths; 6,148 injuries; and 1,023 damaged buildings. The number of reported rapes was 942. Most insightful, however, were the causes of this violence: relatively few cases were related to the state-versus-civilian violence that many public commentators tend to assume is the leading cause of death. The violent deaths recorded by ViCIS in Papua fell into eight categories: popular justice, crime and response, domestic violence, identity or clan violence, political violence, resource-related violence, administrative violence, and others (see Figure 1).

Figure 1. Deaths by Issue

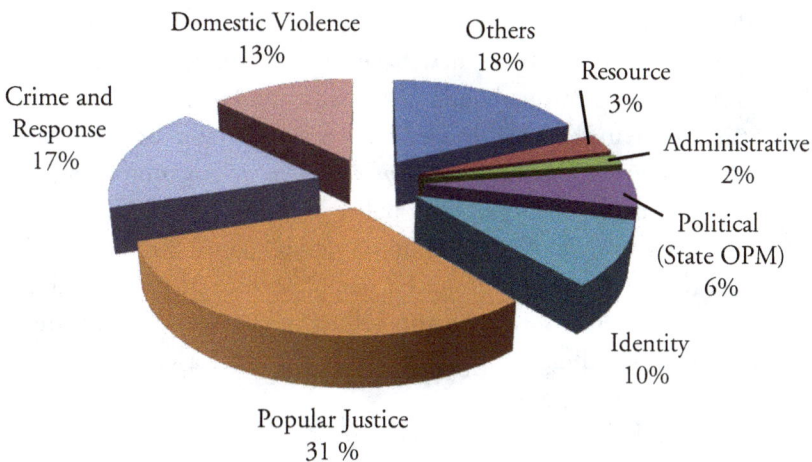

Domestic Violence
13%

Others
18%

Resource
3%

Crime and
Response
17%

Administrative
2%

Political
(State OPM)
6%

Identity
10%

Popular Justice
31 %

Source: ViCIS 2010

Popular justice, or *main hakim sendiri,* resulted in the highest number of killings between 2004 and 2008. There were a number of sub-categories in this type of violence—loss of face, debt, accident, property damage, sexual indiscretion—but all involved vengeance or vigilantism. While witchcraft killings were included in this category, they should be separated into a subset of an overall "violence against women" category, as nearly all the victims are women. In Papua, witchcraft killings are anecdotally as common as they are unreported. Regarding the reasons for the high prevalence of popular justice in Indonesia, most authors have pointed primarily to the public disregard for and endemic corruption within the police force, which is known to demand kickbacks if asked to solve a case. The police, in turn, are often hesitant to investigate killings that they deem to be "local affairs" (Welsh 2008).

> *Endemic corruption within the police force contributes to the high number of popular justice killings*

Crime and response accounted for the second-highest number of deaths. This category mostly consisted of police killings. Importantly, however, police killings were disaggregated from deaths resulting from conflict between the state and the OPM (below). Many of the police killings had a familiar pattern: for instance, thugs shot at an illegal roadblock. To be sure, arbitrary police killings of unarmed suspects are an Indonesia-wide problem; newspapers across the archipelago report with startling regularity about cases in which unarmed suspects were shot by police in the back. Indeed, Jacqui Baker's radio documentary *Eat Pray Mourn: Crime and Punishment in Jakarta* is a compelling exposé on the commonality of such police killings.[15] ViCIS did not report on the ethnicity of perpetrators or victims. Thus, further analysis of SNPK data is needed. Should a preponderance of police killings involve non-Papuan security actors killing indigenous Papuans, then many of those killings might reasonably fit under a category other than "crime and response."

Domestic violence generated twice the number of casualties that vertical conflict between the OPM and TNI did. Alcohol is a contributing factor. This category included the killings of women and children—and, more uncommonly, of men. The category of **identity violence**, for its part, mostly related to clan and other sectarian violence. Nearly all of the 2004–2008 killings in this category can be attributed to clan conflict in Mimika. Ideally, this category would also require some significant disaggregation: in ViCIS, it included killings related to ethnicity, religion, migration, and gender.

Crucially for the argument developed in this study, **political violence**, of which both state-OPM killings and election violence are a subset, represented only 6 percent of recorded killings. Nearly all 2004–2008 deaths occurred in Puncak Jaya. ViCIS did not disaggregate these deaths by civilians, soldiers, OPM, or police, and so the deaths of state security actors fell within this subset as well. As with other categories in the ViCIS survey, the "political violence" category would ideally need further disaggregation[16] in order to give a clearer image of the number of civilians killed by security actors. Finally, additional categories were **resource conflict** (land, natural resources, industrial, and labor actions) and **administrative conflict** (corruption and administrative redistricting, for instance). Of recorded killings, 18 percent fell into the **others** category, which comprised incidents that did not relate to preassigned categories because of either a lack of detail—a body found with stab wounds, but where nothing else was known—or reportage of murders where no reason was given in the report.

The ViCIS death categorizations are equally insightful (see Figure 2). *Assault* was defined as a one-sided attack from an individual or group against another individual or group, where the latter was defenseless/not resisting, and the attacker/victim ratio was under three-to-one. If the ratio was equal to or higher than three-to-one, the ViCIS categorized the killing as a *lynching* (*pengeroyokan*). A *fight* was defined as a two-sided incident involving a minimum of two and a maximum of ten individuals. A fight involving over ten individuals, or a report that didn't specify numbers but referred to "*kelompok*" or "*massa*" (a large crowd), was categorized as a *group clash*. As can be seen in Figure 2, the vast majority of all violence took the form of assaults (69 percent), followed by group clashes, fights, other forms, and lynchings.

The regional distribution of deaths between 2004 and 2008 dispels the widespread perception of Papua as a territory with ubiquitous patterns of violence. In fact, 80 percent of violence occurred in

Figure 2. Deaths by Form

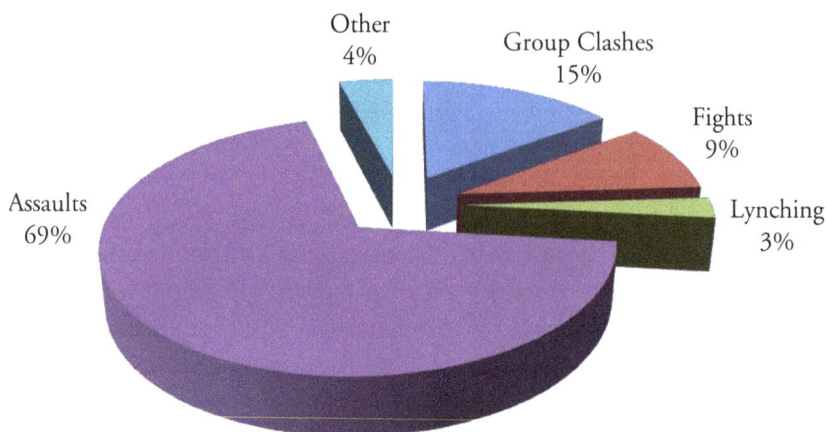

Source: ViCIS 2010

only 9 out of (then) 32 districts (see Figure 3). The most violent were Mimika and Papua's provincial capital Jayapura, with 50 percent of Papua's recorded violent deaths occurring there. Both areas met the "violence epidemic" standard set by the World Health Organization (WHO)—over 10 deaths/year per 100,000 people—matching the levels of Haiti and Liberia. Significantly, Puncak Jaya, which does not reach the WHO threshold, was the only district with significant vertical, separatist conflict. Of the nine districts hosting 80 percent of reported cases of violence, Jayawijaya—a highland district often seen as the epicenter of separatist activity in Papua—was, paradoxically, the *least* violent.

The reportage from the four most violent districts (see Figure 4) lacked information on who actually did the killing; killers were usually classified as *Orang Tak Kenal* (OTK), or unknown persons. In conflict-era Aceh, and at the twilight of the Papuan Spring, OTK was often a code for state killings of civilians. We must assume, then, that at least some of the deaths classified as *other* were indeed victims of state violence. But a cursory review of the raw data indicates that many of the deaths classified as *other* in the most violent districts did not fit such a category. ViCIS found that private companies were most often involved in violent incidents, either as perpetrators or victims. This

Figure 3. Annual Deaths per 100,000 by District, 2004–2008

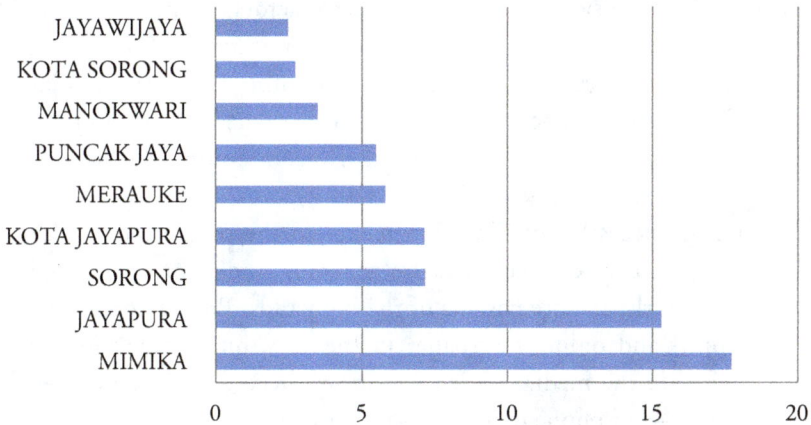

Source: ViCIS 2010

Figure 4. Most Violent Districts and Deaths by Issue

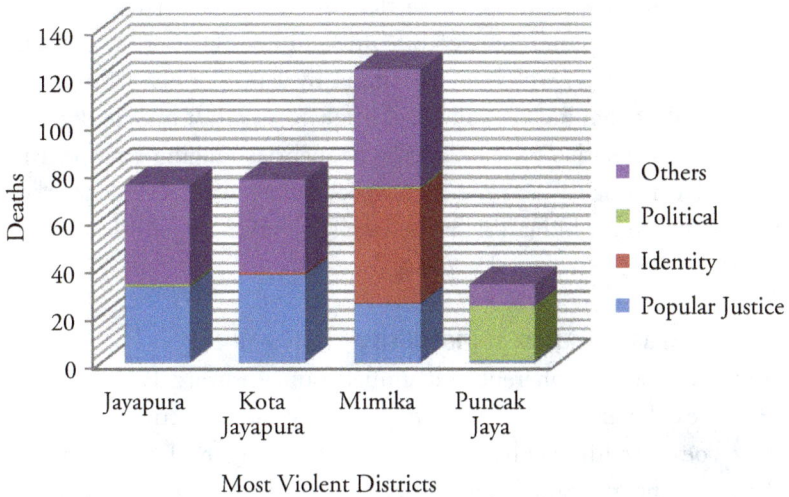

Source: ViCIS 2010

relates to contested concessions for mining, plantation, forestry, and other activities, and the myriad land ownership disputes that accompany such concessions. These private-sector actors are usually aligned with, and empowered by, the state, whose bureaucrats reclassify land and award contracts to private companies without any consultation with the people who actually live on, and use, the land. In southern Papua, land-related abuses are particularly common in the Merauke Integrated Food and Energy Estate (MIFEE).

Another necessary qualification relates to the problem of under-reporting. Violent clan conflicts are generally under- or unreported, especially in the remote corners of the highlands. Project coders read every print and online newspaper in the area, but not all violence makes it into the media. Violence is mostly recorded in areas where journalists—and phone networks—are present. In the author's experience, details on clan killings that occur far from such areas arrive late, if at all. In addition, much of the violence the author has seen or heard of in those corners of Papua with no civil servants, much less journalists, has never been reported. ViCIS, and its successor, the SNPK, are the most comprehensive attempts to quantitatively tally deaths in Papua, and they are the most accurate ones available to researchers. Their conclusions stand in stark contrast to widespread perceptions about state violence being the dominant cause of violent deaths in Papua, but nearly all of the categories, and much of the violence, are built upon the foundations of Johann Galtung's (1969) ideas about structural violence, which were defined by Paul Farmer (2003) as a "broad rubric that includes a host of offensives against human dignity: extreme and relative poverty, social inequalities ranging from racism to gender inequality, and the more spectacular forms of violence that are uncontestedly human rights abuses, some of them punishment for efforts to escape structural violence."

The State as a Source of Insecurity

Indonesia has no coherent and unified policy toward Papua. While there are coherent policies governing security and extractive industries, they coexist with incoherent policies governing health, education, development, migration, and other sectors. Both types of policies—the consistent security approach and the incoherent human development framework—have had negative impacts on indigenous Papuans.

Although the government has consistently and unoriginally cited special autonomy as its Papua policy platform, it has been an unequivocal failure for ordinary Papuans (see below). The policy has only succeeded in the co-option of elites. The government has recognized special autonomy's failings through a 2007 presidential instruction that was quickly forgotten, and the 2011 formation of the Unit for Accelerated Development of Papua and Papua Barat (UP4B), headed by the retired military general Bambang Darmono. But unlike the post-tsunami reconstruction agency in Aceh after which it was nominally modeled—the Agency of the Rehabilitation and Reconstruction for the Region and Community of Aceh and Nias (*Badan Rehabilitasi dan Rekonstruksi Wilayah dan Kehidupan Masyarakat Provinsi Nanggroe Aceh Darussalam Dan Kepulauan Nias Provinsi Sumatera Utara* or BRR)—the UP4B has no authority. Darmono admitted to the weakness of his position: the UP4B could cajole and convince, but not give executive orders.[17] Its mandate was too broad, and it ultimately affected no change.

The civilian and bureaucratic state, then, has played a marginal role in Papua, especially in the remote highlands. As such, the state, through its neglect and tolerance of community-based violence, has been a source of insecurity. The Ministry of Home Affairs, the Vice President's Office, and BAPPENAS all cite the National Community Empowerment Program (*Program Nasional Pemberdayaan Masyarakat,* or PNPM)—along with its successor Village Law Block Grants, or UUDesa—as the primary community development and poverty alleviation device for Papua. But PNPM, and its special autonomy–funded counterpart *Rencana Strategis Pembangunan Kampung* (RESPEK, now *Program Strategis Pembangunan Kampung* or PROSPEK), have had a negligible impact on ordinary Papuans. Many rural Papuans, women especially, even cite the program's harmful impact (Sosa 2014). At the same time, Indonesia's bureaucrats discuss Papua as a problem with no solution, and assignments to Papua, or even desk assignments related to Papua, are considered toxic. But while the civilian element of the state harms Papuan interests through its absence, the military and police arms of

> *The state's military and police arms contribute to insecurity through rent-seeking activities*

the state have contributed to insecurity in Papua through rent-seeking activities in areas where they are present.

The State Security Apparatus as a Source of Insecurity

As of 2011, roughly 14,000 Indonesian military personnel[18] were based in Papua under the auspices of the Cenderawasih Military Command. What sets Papua apart from other Indonesian provinces is the presence of nonorganic[19] security actors, as well as the enhanced presence of the army's Special Forces (*Kopassus*) and the police counterterrorism unit, Densus 88 (ICG 2012). The removal of nonorganic TNI troops from Aceh after the 2005 Helsinki peace agreement resulted in many combat-hardened units being relocated en masse to the Papuan highlands, where they developed a reputation for random violence—so much so that organic TNI troops were afraid of them.[20] Papua also has 14,000 police, as well as civil service security groups attached to local governments, known as the SATPOL PP (*Satuan Polisi Pamong Praja*).

Across Asia's annexed highlands and peripheries, the lowland state's coercive actors have often been the primary (and sometimes only) visible element of the state. As a result, these forces have assumed and exercised extraordinary powers, and they use them widely. Soldiers and police have engaged in extortion, forced labor, rape, killing, and other crimes. Forces often commit such crimes under order, and no sanction greets their acts. However, the extent of brutal military and police crimes differed from area to area. In Yunnan, the suppression of the Panthay Rebellion (1856–1873) approached a state of total annihilation, and imperial China's brutal suppression of rebellion after rebellion in Southwest China created much of the population movement in Zomia over the centuries (Scott 2009). Similarly, the Myanmar military's ruthlessness over dozens of campaigns against highland insurrections has approached the ferocity of Panthay, but not anywhere near the scale. In Indonesia, and in Papua in particular, there have been numerous incidences of atrocity and abuse, and gross human rights violations. But the general insecurity emanating from Indonesia's security forces over time has been much more calculating, and is almost invariably associated with the security forces' extraction of revenue from the territory they control.

Historically, the parasitic behavior of security forces toward communities has been the norm. The state security forces in highland areas of Southeast Asia have all undergone economic evolutions as insurgencies have waned and the state asserted itself. From violent beginnings, in which nonorganic forces extorted, robbed, and terrorized, their activities diversified over time to be more embedded in systems of "acceptable" exchange. In Papua, security actor activities vary by area. Significant differences exist between areas in which organic troops dominate and those showing a heavy nonorganic presence, and between "wet" (i.e., lucrative) areas—especially where unregulated alluvial gold mining occurs, or where the military can present itself as a guarantor of security to a natural resource extraction operation—and "dry" (less lucrative) ones. Nonorganic forces stay in Papua on three- to six-month rotations, and are thus incentivized to earn as much illicit income as possible within their rotation.

It is important to note, however, that security forces have little-to-no presence in Papua's remote corners. Only select areas of Puncak Jaya and the Papuan border with PNG have a large force presence. Security actors are generally limited to areas reachable from barracks by road; as a consequence, most rural Papuans have little day-to-day experience with them. As in the rest of Indonesia, security forces are often more concerned with income generation than security. Despite steady national-level funding increases to the security apparatus, concurrent with an attempt to eliminate extracurricular economic activities, this funding often fails to reach the field.

Security forces have little-to-no presence in Papua's remote corners, where opportunities to generate income are low

The result is that self-financing remains the tenet among local security forces (Baker 2013, Mietzner and Misol 2012). Recent research by Jacqui Baker (2013) illustrates the police off-budget economy in all its tawdry luster. The recent case of a low-level Sorong police officer, Labora Sitorus, who laundered US$129 million in proceeds from smuggling fuel and timber since 2007—coupled with lack of interest in following the trail of funds from him to his superiors—amply demonstrates how embedded these corrupt practices are. Reformers such as Tito Karnavian, onetime police chief of Papua province in the early 2010s, can only have so much impact in this system.

Army and police checkpoints in Papua, as elsewhere in Indonesia (or in rural, highland Myanmar, Arunachal Pradesh, and Nagaland), are often shakedowns, where civilian drivers are fined small amounts for invented infractions. Nonorganic forces join in the rackets. For example, in a 2014 incident, mobile police forces from the greater Jakarta metropolitan area of Depok were sent to Lanny Jaya for "anti-OPM" operations, only to end up shooting a soldier at a checkpoint set up to extort money from civilian drivers (*Jakarta Post* 2014). Despite government efforts to separate TNI from off-budget income streams, the practice continues (Mietzner and Misol 2012), and security actors operate public transport services, shops, vehicle rentals, and private security services. Some also run brothels (Harsono 2007, HRW 2006), sell weapons (*Antara* 2015), and smuggle everything from alcohol to gold.[21] Soldiers often double as motorcycle taxi drivers, while their wives run kiosks. Significantly, the relationship between the various security forces is nearly as contentious as that between opposing clans. The police and the military have competed with one another, including for protection rackets and other illicit income sources, since the police were institutionally removed from the armed forces in 2000. In Papua and elsewhere, propaganda signs advertising different service branches act as territorial demarcation markers, signifying where particular groups exercise control to the disenfranchisement of others.

In some areas, the security forces are part and parcel of the community, with soldier's children going to local schools and camaraderie existing between troops and people. In other areas, the soldiers remain apart, and their interactions with civilians resemble that of any other gang, as they extort communities for funding, food, and laundry. The attitude of troops depends on the local senior officer's disposition and the types of economic activities his forces and their dependents are engaged in. The author has personally witnessed the diversity of the behavior of security forces. In one case, a soldier from Toraja (South Sulawesi)—referred to here as S.—was stationed in Bokondini, Tolikara. His wife ran a kiosk there, while S. purchased a secondhand Toyota Hilux that served as public transport between Wamena and Bokondini. Although S. is a Muslim, his children were enrolled in a private church-run school. From first making his acquaintance in 2011 to the present, the author never saw S. in uniform. He considers himself part of the community, and the community seems to accept S. as well. In contrast, there was also the case Y., a soldier who doubled as a motorcycle taxi driver. He mistook a young indigenous man on a motorcycle for a taxi driver, and thus competition. In September 2011, Y. viciously assaulted the man as he dropped off a friend. These two examples are hardly unique. They represent opposite sides on a pendulum of *average* interactions of soldiers and civilians across Indonesia.

The predatory behavior of security forces in Papua is compounded by their impunity. For instance, soldiers often take on local "wives" for the time of their posting, paying for services such as food, laundry, and sex.[22] Fathers frequently abandon the children of these dalliances when they rotate out, without any legal consequences or obligations. Communities are often pressured to offer such "services" for free; they do so out of fear.[23] One of the worst aspects of the lack of rule of law in Indonesia is that TNI soldiers are subject to civilian laws in theory, but not in practice, and the

> ***The predatory behavior of security forces in Papua is compounded by their impunity***

structure protects its own. Hence, the entire behavioral spectrum—from kindness to sociopathy—can be found in interactions between the TNI and civilians, or between police and civilians. These practices, again, are common across Indonesia. But Papua's unaddressed history of violence, active insurgency, and widespread support for independence mean that all of this behavior, criminal and marginalizing at its best, can also be recast within the question of Papua's place in Indonesia. To be sure, some of these abuses are also committed by Papuans in the security forces against their own people. But the fact that the government of Indonesia has not recognized the intimate relationship between Papua's political problems and the behavior of the security forces, and has failed to mitigate such behavior, indicates the state's callousness, incompetence, or a lack of authority vis-à-vis the TNI and the police forces.

The fragmentation, erratic presence, and economic orientation of many security forces undermine the often-advanced notion of Papua as a tightly controlled "police state" (Elmslie and Webb-Gannon 2013, 144). Indeed, the security apparatus has mostly been unable to use its intelligence services to direct local actors, informants, operations, and forces. Domestic, military, and police intelligence in Papua rarely share information, although Regional Intelligence Communities

(*Komunitas Intelijen Daerah,* or KOMINDA) theoretically exist in order for provincial and district-level representatives to do so. The professionalism of these intelligence actors varies by department. Military intelligence (*Badan Intelijen Strategis,* or BAIS) has the most extensive networks. Kopassus runs an intelligence network separate from BAIS. The presence of the domestic intelligence agency (*Badan Intelijen Negara,* or BIN) is limited: the group's predecessor, BAKIN, had been "frozen out" of Papua by BAIS (Conboy 2004), but this has changed somewhat since the end of the Suharto regime. Police intelligence (*Badan Intelijen Keamanan,* or BAINTELKAM) also has extensive networks in Papua.[24] While some intelligence actors are highly professional, others are amateurish. For instance, intelligence in Papua is often a 9-to-5 activity. Embassy staff researching human rights issues in Papua schedule the most sensitive meetings for very early in the morning because intelligence actors are generally not awake.[25] However, many of the persons targeted by these intelligence bodies display even greater degrees of unprofessionalism, and so the impact, real and potential, remains significant.

State repression is pervasive against groups and activities labeled as separatist. This concerns not only OPM fighters, but also those who raise issues of accountability, human rights, and military impunity. Dissenters are regularly labeled as being involved with the separatist cause. For example, protesting against *adat* (customary) land seizures by companies working in the Merauke Integrated Food and Energy Estate, corrupt practices in local parliaments, or the police beating of a teenager can be interpreted as an insurgent act. But this does not mean that such treatment of dissenting Papuans is characteristic of the entire Papuan territory, nor does it reflect the full spectrum of conflict and violence Papuans are engaged in. While Papuans are regularly subject to harassment and abuse from security forces that suspect the population of separatist sympathies, this occurs mostly in select districts or cities, such as Wamena, Jayapura, Timika, Enarotali, and Dekai. Importantly, vast tracts of Papua are not subject to this state pressure, including nearly the entirety of Papua Barat province.

In the same vein, gross military and police human rights violations toward Papuans have lessened over time—the great exceptions being the periods of state violence that marked the end of the New Order and the end of the Papuan Spring. But a steady stream of violent incidents—beatings, torture, and killings—still occurs, and reminds us of the gulf between the Indonesian government's rhetoric and the actions of its security actors in Papua. The annual US State Department human rights reports (see, for instance, the 2013 edition) highlight the fact that abuses involving security forces are disproportionately frequent in Papua. Crimes against civilians and insurgent suspects continue. Cases include that of Papuan farmers tortured with burning sticks held to their genitalia (*Sydney Morning Herald* 2010, YouTube 2010); of a suspected OPM member interviewed while eviscerated and dying in Puncak Jaya (YouTube 2011, *Jakarta Globe* 2011); of the violent breakup of the Papuan People's Conference in October 2011, and subsequent civilian killings (HRW 2011); of the June 6, 2012, TNI rampage in Wamena (Amnesty International 2012), when soldiers burned close to 100 houses, injured dozens of Papuans and migrants, and officially killed 1; and of the murder of at least 4 Papuan teenagers and wounding of at least 17 others in Enarotali, Paniai, on December 8, 2014 (Kontras 2014). These incidents reveal that security forces in Indonesia view separatism as an insidious threat; that they mythologize contemporary separatism as well as their role in the struggle against it; and

Security forces view separatism as an insidious threat, and mythologize their role in the struggle against it

that they often interweave it with broader conspiracies.[26] But while Indonesian officers believe that their operations contain the threat of separatism, the culture of violence and impunity surrounding these actions have, in fact, increased the likelihood of a "super Santa Cruz" (ICG 2010a) to occur—i.e., an incident similar to the 1991 massacre in East Timor that some Papuan activists hope will serve as the catalyst for their independence struggle.

The examples mentioned above and other similar cases are often offered as tenets of a genocidal policy driven by the Jakarta government (King 2004, King 2006, Monbiot 1989, TAPOL 1983, Wing and King 2005). A more plausible explanation, however, was argued by a prominent specialist on Indonesian politics, Edward Aspinall (2006). According to Aspinall, "authorities are reckless about who might be harmed or killed in pursuit of political or other goals. In Papua, of course, the chief such goal leading to human rights abuses has been an intent to eliminate Papuan nationalism, not to eliminate the Papuans as a group." Similarly, Budi Hernawan has convincingly argued that violence and torture in Papua are utilized by security actors to project the power of the Indonesian state over Papuans accused of "crimes" against it (Hernawan 2013).

While the insecurity caused by security actors is multifaceted, the memory of the past violence of such actors, and the potential for future violence, is a powerful force multiplier. Even friendly interactions between security actors and civilians in Indonesia are marked by the unequal power dynamics at play. Such interactions occur according to each person's place within the state, and the power that they wield or have access to. However, most ordinary Indonesians are scared of the police and the military, and this is not an unreasonable fear. Papuans, in particular, go about their daily lives believing that they could be victims of security actors at any given time. As such, most adopt an air of servility or forced camaraderie in their interactions with security actors. The stress this persistent fear causes in some Papuan communities is often palpable—it surely has indirect effects on relations with neighbors and families, and arguably even contributes to domestic violence and alcohol abuse. No amount of TNI public relations and community outreach will serve to erase this pervasive feeling of dread. Unless the root causes of this anxiety in Papuan society are addressed, the potential for further violence and abuse remains.

The Clan as a Source of Insecurity

Papua's primary marker of identity and a significant source of violence is the clan. Clan conflict and its political manifestations have resulted in casualties of much greater number than vertical conflict between Indonesian security actors and separatists or host populations. The splitting of administrative territories by clans through *pemekaran* is an additional source of insecurity: populations are separated from weak but functioning services in pre-existing districts. These collapsed service systems are typically not reconstituted. Instead, service budgets are absorbed into pre-existing Melanesian systems of exchange, and funds earmarked for health and education are turned into no-show jobs awarded to clan members, cash handouts to families, and electoral slush funds. An example of this pattern is the abovementioned

RESPEK program, the funds of which have been largely unaccounted for (Sosa 2014). These patronage structures are particularly acute in the highlands, with Nduga, Puncak Jaya, Tolikara, and Yahukimo all serving as examples of new districts that failed to uphold basic services. The state's promotion of indigenous elite co-option, regardless of the negative impacts upon ordinary citizens, constitutes a cynical form of conflict resolution: those elites that may have potentially threatened the state are incorporated into the income streams it provides (Aspinall 2009). Indigenous leaders are empowered within very specific parameters, often at the expense of services. This co-option pattern has precedent in Aceh (ibid), as well as northeastern India and insurgent Myanmar.

The divisions this approach has caused within Papuan societies are evident. While much of Papuan civil society has prioritized Papuan rights in the face of a national government that is characterized by abuse or absence, a smaller number of civil society organizations and churches have been increasingly vocal about conflict among indigenous elites that sacrifices the interests of their own people. This is especially evident in Tolikara, a district with clan conflict so pervasive that services barely existed until recently. However, most public attention has been directed toward intra-elite tensions in Jayapura and other towns—tensions that were partly related to the issue of "handing back" special autonomy to the central gov-

> *In Tolikara, clan conflict was so pervasive that services barely existed until recently*

ernment in 2010 (MacLeod 2010). At the grassroots level in the rural highlands, this tension has been less evident. There, services barely existed in the first place, keeping expectations toward government benefits low. In other words, ordinary citizens in these highland communities are less aware that they are being cheated out of institutional state services. The pittances citizens receive in the form of handouts, on the other hand, are seen as a "big man's" culturally obligatory largesse. Similarly, interclan violence is often viewed in the highlands as a normal and culturally sanctioned state of affairs, much in contrast to violence committed by the security forces.

In most cases, violence between clans only comes to the attention of outsiders when it manifests itself in elections that have become proxy battles of older struggles. Across the Papuan provinces, decentralization has turned many *bupatis* (district leaders) into feudal lords who often spend more time in Jayapura or Jakarta than in the areas they are supposed to govern. Occupying and distributing both civil servant positions and elected posts in local legislatures, as well as awarding contracts, are important parts of operating and perpetuating the pre-existing patronage system. Clans have therefore co-opted, rather than adapted to, electoral politics, using Indonesia's vacuous political parties as vehicles of competition. This has led to a number of cases in which clan conflict occurred in the disguise of electoral races. For instance, a Golkar legislator was beaten to death by a mob of Partai Demokrat supporters in early 2013 in Tolikara (*Bintang Papua* 2014). That killing was a continuation of the fight between the Bogoga and Wanui clans (Anderson 2014d) that had begun with the 2012 *bupati*

> *Local electoral violence with high casualty rates is not unusual in Papua*

election between incumbent district leader and Bogoga leader Jon Tabo and a Wanui electoral challenger. This conflict led to 11 killings, dozens wounded, and dozens of homes burned. In Puncak in July 2011, two clans seeking the Gerindra franchise to back their district leader candidacies went to war with one another. In the first week of the conflict, 23 people were killed, dozens were wounded, and numerous homes were destroyed. Neither "won" the *bupati* seat (Arios 2012). Similarly, inter-Nduga clan struggles over the contested 2013 *bupati* election have led to dozens of deaths in the highlands and as far away as Sentani.[27] Local electoral violence with such high casualty rates is not unusual in Papua, but it is unprecedented elsewhere in Indonesia.

Interclan violence can occur at the slightest accusation. In Tolikara, a clan war erupted in August 2011 between the Woraga and Tiyoga clans when a 15-year-old disabled girl died, and a woman employed by a local church was accused of witchcraft and murdered by the girl's family. Within days, 19 people (including a priest who attempted to mediate) were killed with knives, spears, and other weaponry. This clan war did not even make the newspapers, even though it ultimately required security forces to mediate between the clans.[28] In Nalca, Yahukimo, a clan war has lasted from the summer of 2011 to the present, with trails between villages destroyed and ambushes common.

Every boy above the age of 10 is armed.[29] That conflict, previously held in check by an uneasy truce, was touched off when a mentally disabled teenager sexually assaulted a woman. The church, for its part, is incorporated into clan identities in remote areas to the extent that parishes occasionally go to war with one another. In Tolikara, the author was confused by the attempted murder of a church leader by another church leader in 2013, until it became clear that it had nothing to do with the church. Ecclesiastical battles have resulted in church burnings, assaults, and killings. A notable aspect of this and other forms of clan violence is that it is targeted: persons not affiliated with warring sides are not killed unless they interfere.

Separatist Groups as a Source of Insecurity

Rich contrasts can be found in the relative successes and failures of highland insurgencies against newly independent states. Unlike the *Organisasi Papua Merdeka* (OPM, or Free Papua Organization), Myanmar's Kachin Independence Organization (KIO) and a multitude of other highland separatist groups initially managed to create parallel states. Kachin is one of the best organized: at one stage, the KIO ran 119 primary schools, 10 middle schools, 5 high schools, and 2 hospitals with operation theaters and X-rays (Lintner 1997). KIO services were partially funded by extralegal natural resource and other taxes, which continue to be levied and opaquely allocated (Dean 2012, 121). Taxes on jadeite provide up to half of the KIO's operating budget (*New York Times* 2014).[30] The Communist Party of Burma (CPB) was also initially successful in its state-building endeavors that began in 1946; the movement, however, shrank after financial support from China ended in 1978. The CPB derived significant income from poppy cultivation and heroin processing, especially after it was reconstituted into the United Wa State Party (UWSP) in 1989 (Lintner 1990).[31] In Nagaland, Northeast India, insurgents who rose up against the Indian state in the 1950s soon developed comprehensive extortion and protection rackets, and engaged in fratricidal wars—more so than they either fought the state or provided services (Chasie and Hazarika 2009; Singh 2004; Lintner 2011; Upadhyay 2009, 257). They, and other insurrectionists in Northeast India, espouse ideologies to mask the economic rationales of their current activities, and they act as shadow security forces, "descending, despite high-sounding ideals and rhetoric, into a criminalized oligarchy" (Chasie and Hazarika 2009, 27).

Arguably, one of the main reasons for the inability of the OPM to become a viable foe of the government of Indonesia is the egalitarian nature of Melanesian societies. Given this egalitarianism, OPM's initial administrative hierarchy quickly collapsed. In addition, unlike its Kachin counterpart, it provided no services and lacked a plausible post-independence state framework. Thus, the OPM never acted as a parallel state. And while the OPM was initially a political wing, with the *Tentara Pembebasan Nasional* (TPN) designed only as the OPM's armed wing, the TPN emerged as the more active group. However, for much of its existence, it has lacked arms, training, and numbers, and has generally consisted of sparsely armed rural cells. Unlike GAM, which had a thorough extralegal taxation system (Anderson 2013c, Aspinall 2009, Schulze 2004), the OPM was initially unable to derive income from the "assets" existing in the areas its factions sought to control. This pattern is only slowly changing. In Paniai, for example, OPM factions have been known to establish toll checkpoints and to levy taxes on government projects or businesses. In the same vein, mining and agribusiness endeavors in Jayawijaya, Lanny Jaya, Paniai, and Puncak Jaya have, in recent years, been forced to pay off local OPM officials. However, this money is typically absorbed into the personal networks of factions, and does not strengthen the OPM as a Papua-wide, effective organization.

The last OPM leader of cross-regional prominence was Kelly Kwalik; he was killed in Timika in 2009. Only a few notable OPM-affiliated groups, namely Goliath Tabuni's faction in Tingginambut and Purom Wenda's in Lanny Jaya (the two are rivals), pose a threat to state actors in their territory. With the exception of these and a few other local factions, the OPM's role in the independence discourse continues to diminish. Instead, the lead role in this discussion has shifted to the West Papua National Committee (*Komisi Nasional Papua Barat*, or KNPB). The KNPB organized its first protests in 2009, and it has strong links to exiled independence activist Benny Wenda, as well as Wenda-affiliated entities such as International Parliamentarians for West Papua and International Lawyers for West Papua. The KNPB claims to be a Papua-wide movement, but it has not yet reached a presence across the two provinces. Initially, it had little representation outside of Jayapura and select parts of the highlands, such as Wamena and Pyramid. However, the organization appears to be expanding as a result of ongoing abuses in Papua's highlands, with widespread pro-KNPB graffiti indicative of popular sentiment.

The KNPB has categorically claimed to be nonviolent, but this is open to question. In fact, some speculate that its previous leadership was behind a series of migrant murders in Jayapura in 2012, which underlay the group's then-strategy to trigger a response from state security actors (ICG 2012, *Suara Pembaruan* 2011). These killings halted when KNPB Deputy Mako Tabuni was killed by security forces on June 14, 2012 (ibid.). But Tabuni's death hardly ended the group's domination of the independence discussion. Indeed, the movement seems to have matured over time, with current leader Victor Yiemo transcending the popularity of his deceased and jailed predecessors. The group's current activities are focused on political pressure to achieve a referendum on independence; should these efforts turn out to be unsuccessful, however, the KNPB views future armed action as an option. The KNPB's uncom-

> *The independence group KNPB appears to be expanding as a result of ongoing abuses in Papua's highlands*

promising stance has much appeal among young Papuans who are frustrated by other independence leaders (especially the older exiles), disgusted by their own co-opted elites, and hateful of a national government that, in their view, provides them with nothing. The KNPB's membership—and its popular sentiment for a radical solution to the independence question—are likely to grow further. Thus, while vertical conflict between the state and pro-independence groups are far from being the largest source of fatalities in Papua, it remains a significant contributor to insecurity.

Migration as a Source of Insecurity

Under the transmigration program, which began with the Dutch but was accelerated by Suharto's New Order regime, the poor from densely populated Java, Madura, and Bali were relocated to Kalimantan, Papua, and Sumatra. For Papuans, transmigration constituted the arrival of the army and heavy machinery, the razing of forests, and the construction of settlements that excluded them. Traditional land ownership was not honored. Instead, land was seized without compensation, an act that has not been forgotten. The government presented transmigration as an exercise in both poverty alleviation and outer-island development, mixed with social engineering elements: by comingling peoples, transmigration promoted an "Indonesian" identity. But transmigration served to redistribute, rather than alleviate, poverty. Many transmigrants now work in Papua as porters and motorcycle taxi drivers, far from the promises of fast material advancement that the government promoted. In terms of the social engineering component, the program smacked of James C Scott's notion of engulfment (Scott 2009, 40): that is, loyal (read: docile) populations with an existing "Indonesian" identity were sent to areas where such identity was lacking among indigenous peoples. Transmigrants were then put to work in such industries as construction and palm oil, setting them apart from the local population. They felt under threat from Papuans and sought protection from the local security apparatus, further branding them as outsiders.

The official government transmigration program was significantly reduced in 1998 (McGibbon 2004), and was halted by the Wahid government in 2000 (ICG 2006). Theoretically, transmigration is still possible. For transmigrants to arrive in Papua, the provincial government must request them and must cooperate in their resettlement. However, this is politically unpalatable for any indigenous governor. Instead, spontaneous migration occurs. The archipelago's poor are drawn to the area by economic growth driven by extractive industries and a construction boom, which is fueled by special autonomy and the creation of new districts. In order to control and manage migration, the Papua provincial government has passed Regulation 11/2013, but it contains no framework for enforcement.

The archipelago's poor are drawn to the area by extractive industries and a construction boom

Papuans—along with Kachins, Tibetans, Naga, and others—know that uncontrolled in-migration will reduce them to minorities, with their cultures and lands subsumed by newcomers. Rich historical precedents exist, such as Manchu/Qing settlement of Han Chinese colonists and soldiers in Southwest China (Unger 1997). Indeed, Han settlement into areas where they are not a majority has been a Chinese government policy that transcends ideologies, and its continuity from empire to republic to communist dictatorship to the present appears unbroken. Significantly, the greater the disruption of the previous demographic status quo, the greater the volatility, as is demonstrated by contemporary anti-state violence in Xinjiang and an epidemic of self-immolations in Tibet.

Demographic and economic data from Papua illustrates the explosive nature of migration as a source of insecurity. According to the 2010 census, Papua's population was 3.6 million: 2.83 million in Papua province and 760,000 million in Papua Barat. The census reported that the migrant population of Papua Barat stood at 47.7 percent; in Papua province, it was 23.8 percent. Migrants were the majority in urban areas. But this data has been contested. Jim Elmslie at the University of Sydney estimated that, based on historical growth rates, the 2010 population of Papua was 52 percent Papuan to 48 percent non-Papuan (Elmslie 2010).[32] Contrasting the 2000 population of Papua (at 2.2 million) with the 2010 population (3.6 million) is telling: the population has increased by 62 percent since transmigration ended, but only a distinctly small percentage of this population increase can be attributed to indigenous births (which have been declining, especially in the highlands, since the 1980s).[33] The combined current GDRP for Papua province and Papua Barat was 114,606 trillion rupiah or US$12,613 billion[34] in 2010[35]; per capita GDRP was US$3,509, which is impressive compared to the nationwide average of under US$2,500 (Badan Pusat Statistik 2013). The majority of GDRP undoubtedly accrues in the hands of elites, but what does accrue with ordinary workers is concentrated in the urban, migrant areas that host the majority of economic activity (the 2010 urban population of Papua province was 41.5 percent, and in Papua Barat 44.4 percent).

In Papua, as in many other areas around the world, resentment toward migrants is widespread. In the view of the local population, migrants generally do not respect, much less adapt to, local cultures, and indigenous peoples have difficulty competing against migrants for jobs or business opportunities. Discrimination occurs on both sides: indigenous citizens tend to exclude migrants from many aspects of daily life, while migrants prefer to hire other migrants in their businesses. Migrants historically dominate local markets: the Marwaris and Biharis dominate in Naga and other areas of Northeast India; the Chinese in Kachin; the Han Chinese in Tibet; and the Bataks, Bugis, Butonese, and Makassarese in Papua. In Papuan stereotyping and in some foreign interpretations of migration in Papua, migrants are assumed to be mostly Javanese Muslims, which was true under transmigration when they constituted the bulk of settlers (Farhadian 2005, 62). Since that program ended, however, migrants are primarily Ambonese, Bugis, Butonese, Minahasans, Makassarese, Bataks, Minangkabau, Timorese, and others. Many are Christians and worship in Papuan churches, although many ethnic churches—such as Batak Protestant churches—have increasingly established themselves in Papua. While such migration patterns are a significant source of insecurity in Papua, the large-scale violence that has accompanied migration-related demographic changes in other areas of Asia has not yet occurred, with the exception of the Dani uprising in 1977–1978. This does not mean, however, that it won't occur in the future.

Other Sources of Everyday Insecurity

In their daily lives, Papuans deal with mundane dimensions of insecurity that, over time, have catastrophic consequences. For instance, health and education services barely exist outside of migrant-dominated towns, creating constant threats to human security. In the countryside, a significant number of women with pregnancy complications die because there is no health clinic present; or because it is closed or unstaffed; or because there is no road connecting the places where these women live to a functioning health clinic; or because it is impossible to call a health worker for instruction; or because of a combination of all of these reasons. Similarly, Papua's high HIV (human immunodeficiency virus) transmission rates and the spread of MDR (multidrug-resistant) and XDR (extensively drug-resistant) tuberculosis pose an overwhelming challenge to Papua's dysfunctional health system (Anderson 2014a). This health crisis is compounded by the generally poor state or absence of other logistical services. Transportation infrastructure remains

In their daily lives, Papuans deal with mundane insecurities that lead to catastrophic consequences

severely underdeveloped, and few of Papua's major towns are connected to one another by road. Moreover, logistics costs increase the prices of basic goods by up to tenfold, and much of Papua, especially the highlands, does not have mobile phone networks or landlines.

In addition to the structural violence institutionalized by poverty and poor health services, a host of other sources of insecurity persist. Rural roads are plagued with opportunistic civilian roadblocks that often trigger conflict. Migrant-driven minibuses ride with a *konek*, a local to negotiate the price. If disagreements arise, cars are sometimes burned, causing more serious incidents. Smaller roadblocks abound, many manned by drunks who attempt to push drivers from their motorcycles when they try to pass without giving a few thousand rupiah. Again, many of these cases have spilled over into mob or clan violence. Furthermore, accusations of black magic and the demand for restitution payments constitute a daily form of unpoliced extortion. Likewise, intra-Papuan sexual assault and domestic violence occur at epidemic levels, as shown by the ViCIS data. Finally, the structural failures of the education system have guaranteed the continuation of indigenous subsistence employment, which in turn fuels the collective sense of marginalization and discrimination by wealthier migrants. That Papua is so resource-wealthy, and yet so few of its indigenous population benefit from this, forms the nucleus of the region's insecurity. This insecurity will persist until either corrective measures occur, or until all resources are gone.

Distorted Images of Papua

The real Papua—chaotic, inequitable, and conflict-ridded though it may be—is more nuanced than the sinister image promoted by some independence activists and their supporters. As one analysis suggested, "genocide is taking place in Indonesian-controlled West Papua" (Elmslie and Webb-Gannon 2013, 143). Similarly, a Yale Law School report from 2004 asserts that "evidence strongly indicates" that "the Indonesians" are inflicting upon the indigenous Papuan population "conditions of life calculated to bring about its physical destruction" (Brundige et al. 2004, 59). The report cites, for example, that "the Indonesian military has regularly engaged in the destruction of property and crops belonging to and cultivated by the indigenous people of West Papua." This type of destruction, when engaged in with the requisite intent, constitutes "deliberately inflicting conditions of life calculated to destroy a group in whole or in part" (ibid, 68). The report also stated that "Indonesia's transmigration program seems clearly to constitute the deliberate infliction of 'conditions of life calculated to destroy' West Papuans" (ibid, 69). An illustrative column in the *Guardian* (UK) offers an easily digestible platitude to explain the world's indifference: "The cultural genocide and mass murder is (sic) widely ignored by the international community. Why? Because Papua is cursed with resources, and international corporations are making a killing" (Griffiths 2011).

In this view, Papua is a tightly controlled colony, closed to outsiders and run by an omnipotent security apparatus that is committing genocide, where indigenous human rights activists bravely expose Indonesia's crimes to the outside world and are hunted down and killed. In the midst of this genocide, all-powerful corporations loot Papua of its wealth. Indonesia, in this discourse, is run by a "centralised Javanese regime" (Saltford 2000, 5). Journalist Mark Aarons even claimed that Indonesia was a "West Javanese empire" (Australian Broadcasting Corporation 2006). George Darroch, from his experience with Papua independence activists in Australia and New Zealand, notes that many of his research interviewees "have expressed the idea that Papua is dominated by 'Java' and 'Javanese,' and that Indonesia is a 'Javanese empire' rather than a multi-ethnic nation. This view is of Indonesia as a 'Jakarta regime,' based around Java and operated by 'Asians'" (Darroch 2009, 21).

Aspirant Papuan diaspora leaders and their local supporters consistently promote this image. According to Benny Wenda, "few Papuans manage to get out of West Papua alive to share their story" (Wenda 2013). He asserts that "there's a silent genocide going on in West Papua" (Hyslop 2011). Independence leader Forkorus Yaboisembut doesn't explicitly state that genocide is occurring, but he alludes to it: "It cannot be said that, according to the definition of genocide, that is what is happening, but the situation is moving in that direction" (JUBI 2011). Non-Indonesian supporters of Papuan independence consistently use the word "genocide," while offering the caveat that it might not be occurring, through provocative report and editorial titles such as "Genocide in West Papua?" (Wing and King, 2005) and "On the Brink of Genocide" (Leadbeater 2005). Wenda's lawyer, Jennifer Robinson, warns that "Yale and Sydney Universities report that the situation is approaching genocide" (Robinson 2012). Importantly, reports often make broad assertions without substantiating their "evidence." For example, one University of Sydney report suggested that "young West Papuan girls are now being enslaved sexually by the military during their operations in the remotest areas of West Papua" (Wing and King 2005, 11).

In Australia and New Zealand, this lobbyism is often falling on fertile grounds, with generally disinterested populations holding an intrinsic suspicion of Indonesia due to issues ranging from the current influx of refugees to Australia via Indonesia to Jakarta's brutal 25-year occupation of East Timor. The cause of West Papuan independence is popular in Fiji, Papua New Guinea, the Solomon Islands, and Vanuatu.

The genocide claim in particular deserves close scrutiny. The United Nations defines genocide as "any of the following acts committed with intent to destroy, in whole or in part, a national, ethnical, racial, or religious group, as such: (a) Killing members of the group; (b) Causing serious bodily or mental harm to members of the group; (c) Deliberately inflicting on the group conditions of life calculated to bring about its physical destruction in whole or in part; (d) Imposing measures intended to prevent births within the group; (e) Forcibly transferring children of the group to another group" (UN 1948). While Indonesia's actions in Papua have clearly led to the death, and "serious bodily or mental harm" of Papuans, it is difficult to argue that this was done with the goal of exterminating Papuans as an ethnic group. If Indonesia intended to exterminate Papuans, it would have installed the logistical and transport infrastructure to handle the mobilization that genocide requires.

It is difficult to argue that Indonesia's actions were meant to exterminate Papuans as an ethnic group

Moreover, it could have easily done so in the Suharto era, when Cold War realpolitik and inadequate communications links to the outside world would have supported such an effort. Indeed, the government's ability to mobilize proxies to exterminate a minimum of 500,000 leftists in 1965–1966 amply demonstrates the capacity of the Indonesian state for mass killings if it wished to conduct them.

However, there is no evidence of genocide, or even targeted killing of adult males. There are neither gender or age disparities among the indigenous population to indicate this (Upton 2009), nor is a population decline evident. Cited death tolls (100,000 to 500,00) have no established basis. The earliest estimates cite 100,000 fatalities, often attributed to an Amnesty International (AI) report from the mid-1980s (see, for example, Griffiths 2011). Current AI staff and others working in AI at the time of alleged publication are not aware of this report.[36] The author has also not managed to locate it. The earliest source still available is TAPOL's *West Papua: The Obliteration of a People*, which stated that "estimates of the numbers killed or who have died as a result of Indonesian repression, suppression or neglect range from 100,000 to 150,000 since 1963" (TAPOL 1983, viii). The source is not referenced. Moreover, the book's 1988 edition alleged that cysticercosis, a parasitic tissue infection transmitted by pig tapeworms, was intentionally introduced to infect indigenous Papuans, while not affecting Muslim (non–pork consuming) transmigrants (TAPOL 1988, 59). The 1983 TAPOL figure is the foundation for nearly all the works that allege genocide in Papua, including a widely cited Yale Law School report (Brundige et al. 2004)[37] that contains striking inaccuracies (ICG 2006), including the false description of a October 2000 massacre of migrants by a Papuan mob in Wamena as a TNI massacre of Papuans.

This highly speculative treatment of the death toll issue raises the question of what the real number is. Thus, more systematic exercises to establish the qualitative and quantitative dimensions of the human rights violations in Papua are urgently needed. The work of the Asian Human Rights Commission (AHRC 2013) in the Baliem Valley particular to the 1977–78 Dani uprising is one example of such a systematic approach. The same applies to the work of Human Rights Watch (HRW), which has delivered regular and substantiated updates on the human rights situation in Papua. At this point, therefore, all numbers regarding the total death toll are only conjecture. Part of the problem is that the Indonesian government has made research into these issues in Papua difficult, especially for organizations such as the AHRC and HRW. In fact, it would be in the interest of forward-thinking elements of the Indonesian government to allow for such research, because the fact that there *is* a significant death toll from Papua's incorporation cannot be disputed. Incongruously, it has been the government's defensive and ineptly argued positions that have lent credibility to higher fatality figures.

In order to strengthen the genocide claim, some Papuan activists have tried to "localize" its definition, and to broaden its scope. According to Benny Giay, "The word 'genocide' is usually defined by institutions and powerful states that are perpetrators of violence. West Papuans have the right to define this word for ourselves. We have experienced a genocide during the last 40 years of Indonesian rule" (Kirksey 2012, 225). In this context, many Papuans believe that the spread of HIV[38] and family planning are part of a genocidal strategy. Similarly, Jim Elmslie has argued that migration to Papua constitutes genocide (Elmslie and Webb-Gannon 2013, 158). But Papua received only 220,256 migrants from the official government transmigration program between 1964 and 2000 (Herawati 1998, 79). Had the New Order government intended to radically alter Papuan demographics

> *To strengthen the genocide claim, some activists have tried to localize its definition and broaden its scope*

by dilution with a more pliable population, it could have resettled far greater numbers of transmigrants. Interestingly, Elmslie does not assert genocide in Kalimantan and other transmigration recipient areas, which witnessed much greater population movements. Finally, Elmslie and Webb-Gannon also cite indigenous Christian children sent to Islamic boarding schools in Java for conversion[39] as evidence of genocide under clause "e" of the UN's 1948 definition of genocide (Elmslie and Webb-Gannon 2013, 152). However, the acts of a few Islamic boarding schools, aided by indigenous highland Walesi Muslims, are not indicative of government policy to convert Papuans. In addition, the ease with which Christian missionaries have been allowed to enter Papua moots that argument.

The misleading genocide claim is interdependent with the equally problematic assertion that Papua is closed.[40] As mentioned above, the Indonesian government places restrictions on foreign journalists and some nongovernmental organizations (NGOs), including international human rights groups.[41] But Indonesian—including Papuan—journalists are generally not limited by such restrictions. The online news source JUBI, for example, produces comprehensive reportage across Papua, much of it focused on corruption and state abuses. Foreign journalists heavily rely on these local journalists as sources. In the same vein, tourist permits are also easily obtained. An "undercover" ABC news team (Australian Broadcasting Corporation 2012) travelled to Papua on tourist visas, as did two French journalists who were arrested in Wamena in 2014. Technically Indonesians, including many journalists and activists who are passionate defenders of Papuan rights, can travel anywhere in Papua. Some NGOs and UN agencies also operate in Papua, although some—such as Cordaid and the International Committee of the Red Cross—were later pressured to leave. The international human rights group Peace Brigades International (PBI) was allowed by the government to operate in Papua, and when PBI decided to close the Indonesia program in 2010, it did so due to internal managerial issues rather than government actions.[42]

Clearly, some Papuan independence activists and their academic allies propagate the notion of genocide to bring international attention to their cause, and to increase mobilization in Papua itself. To that end, the histories of literal genocides are implicitly imposed upon the Papuan model. But the Papuan case is very dissimilar to that of the European Jews, Ottoman Armenians, Rwandan Tutsis, Bosnian Muslims, Cambodians, or Iraqi Kurds. Many Papuans have been convinced by pro-independence figures, diaspora leaders, and select foreign supporters that independence is warranted and achievable, and that their situation—which, in reality, constitutes one chapter of many within the vast history of state colonization of highland and peripheral areas—is genocidal in nature. The situation of Papuans, while grotesque and cruel, is a common feature in the experience of indigenous peoples as conquerors break their worlds. A word sufficient to capture the enormity of that loss has not yet been coined; the term "genocide," however, can't fill that vacancy.

Conclusion and Recommendations

Rural Papua is distinguished from other areas of Southeast Asia because of its extreme nondevelopment. The majority of Papuans support independence because they see no benefit from the state; they experience its abuses or its neglect, or both at the same time. In the future, the notion of independence may become an increasingly vague abstraction. But for now, many Papuans cling to the idea of *Merdeka* desperately, because they see no alternate way to improve their lives and the lives of their children. Health and education services barely exist; most rural indigenous livelihoods are at subsistence levels; and the "rule of law" is an alien concept in an area in which local extortionists wear military and police uniforms. Meanwhile, Papuan elites, especially in the highlands, have been co-opted by the trinity of decentralization, administrative splitting, and special autonomy. The latter, claimed as an example of state munificence, benefits the political elites in Jakarta more than it does Papuans. This is because special autonomy allows the national-level government to blame co-opted indigenous elites, and incapable civil servants, for the failures that the Indonesian state has caused through decades of callousness and neglect.

The pervasive and multifaceted insecurity in contemporary Papua, however, remains poorly understood. Much of this insecurity stems from the lack of a functioning state rather than from its overwhelming presence. Many areas of rural and highland Papua remain trapped in an era of absorption and incorporation that other territories of Indonesia and Southeast Asia went through generations earlier. Abuses against indigenous Papuans continue. But with the exception of irregular acts of state violence, such as the killings in Enarotali in 2014 and Wamena in 2012, the everyday abuses of security actors toward civilians in Papua are not fundamentally dissimilar from military and police transgressions in other provinces—especially those in which weak governance

> *Abuses by security forces are interpreted within the context of an unaddressed history of humiliation, racism, and killing*

and security problems persist. In Papua, however, abuses by security forces occur—and are invariably interpreted—within the context of an unaddressed history of humiliation, racism, and killing. Because of this unreckoned history, Papua's problems cannot be considered as simple development deficiencies. Providing services to Papuans and protecting them from depredations are essential to the solution of the area's protracted conflict, but these measures need to go hand in hand with other, more political steps. This concluding section evaluates some of the ongoing initiatives for peace in Papua, and offers some additional recommendations.

The Papua Road Map, Dialogue, and Reconciliation

One of the most frequently discussed reform blueprints for Papua has been the "policy road map" developed by the Indonesian Institute of Sciences (LIPI). Issued in 2008 for the government's consideration, the LIPI road map aptly grouped the causes of Papua's multitude of conflicts under four categories: first, marginalization of and discrimination against indigenous Papuans; second, the failure of development; third, contending accounts of the history of Papua's incorporation into Indonesia; and fourth, state violence against Papuans (LIPI 2008). Corresponding to these four problems, LIPI proposed a four-pronged policy platform, focusing on the following: first, recognition of Papuans as the traditional owners of the land; second, a new paradigm of development focusing on Papuans; third, dialogue in order to reach agreement on a shared history; and fourth, reconciliation through justice for the victims of past abuses (ibid).

Despite initial support for the road map in some government circles and civil society, the Yudhoyono administration ignored LIPI's recommendations. Dialogue and reconciliation were the most contentious issues: the initiation of the former would upend the national myth that Papuans continued to suffer under the Dutch until they were freed by Indonesia, while the promotion of the latter included the planned establishment of a truth and reconciliation commission and human rights courts—both of which threaten the vested interests of key actors in Indonesia's political elite and security forces. The government also rejected the LIPI recommendation for a neutral third party to mediate a dialogue, viewing such an idea as a further, unacceptable "internationalization" of an intrinsically Indonesian issue. Nevertheless, LIPI continued to advocate for the road map, as did many civil society representatives who believed that it was the clearest way forward for Papua. But the policy blueprint was finally dealt a deathblow in October 2011 when independence advocates hijacked the LIPI-facilitated Papua Peace Network meeting in Jayapura and provocatively proposed a "dialogue" in the form of an English-language international tribunal where the Indonesian government would be forced to argue its "case."[43]

The road map remains the most pragmatic path toward peace and justice in Papua, and LIPI has expressed its intention to reinvigorate it. But the road map may have a better chance if the four prongs were to progress independently from one another, and if LIPI were to concentrate on facilitating ownership and development while leaving dialogue and reconciliation processes to others. While LIPI has commendably sought to act as an impartial facilitator, it remains an Indonesian government entity. The process of pursuing dialogue and reconciliation might be better served if it were handed over to a coalition led by churches from Papua and other areas of Indonesia: for instance, GIDI, KINGMI, and the Office for Justice and Peace of the Catholic Church in Papua. In this coalition, respected Papuan rights advocates such as Benny Giay, Neles Tebay, Dorman Wandikbo, Jan Christian Warinussy, and Socratez Yeoman could assume leadership roles, in concert with trusted outside interlocutors such as Budi Hernawan and Jacky Manuputty. The coalition wouldn't have to involve government in its earlier stages. Instead, it should first grow so large that the security forces cannot disrupt it, and government will have no choice but to engage with the coalition. The most important aspect of such an exercise is that it must not be hijacked by diaspora utopians. While truth-telling and acknowledgment of suffering are crucial and indispensible goals of such a coalition, the process itself is not a referendum, and the language used must be Indonesian.

Papuans don't only need to have their suffering recognized, they need institutional reforms to mitigate further abuses

Security Sector Reform

In order to have a chance of succeeding, reconciliation requires continued security sector reform (SSR). Papuans don't only need to have their suffering recognized; they need institutional reforms that at least mitigate the likelihood of further abuses in the future. SSR began after Suharto's fall with the separation of the police from the military, the end of the military's sociopolitical role, the removal of allocated seats for the military in the parliament, and the theoretical subservience of TNI to a civilian defense minister (Mietzner 2006). The military was also weaned from its businesses and foundations—activities that were widely seen to fuel abuses (HRW 2006). These were all steps in the direction of a theoretically reformed Indonesian military that would act as the implementer of civilian-led policies. But in reality, these reforms have not been institutionalized (Mietzner 2011), and the military is still a policymaker that wields significant power down to the village level across Indonesia. Most importantly, the territorial command structure remains in place (Mietzner 2006), serving the role of internal surveillance and control rather than protection from external threats. Similarly, while the TNI budget has climbed significantly since the early 2010s in order to ensure that territorial units no longer need to self-finance, that doesn't mean that rent-seeking has stopped. Indeed, with the formal phasing out of military businesses and foundations, the raising of TNI off-budget funds by units and individual officers has increasingly shifted into illicit zones of racketeering and other illegal or semi-illegal activities. Papua, with its natural resource extraction industry and lucrative conflict economy, has provided a fertile ground for these military rent-seeking operations. Without accelerated reform, the economic motivations for military abuses in Papua are unlikely to disappear or even just diminish.

Without accelerated reform, the economic motivations for military abuses in Papua are unlikely to disappear

As important as military reform is police reform, both at the national level and in Papua itself. Police reform in Papua began during the tenure of the regional police chief Made Pastika (2001–2003) and continued under later chiefs, most notably Tito Karnavian (2012–2014). Both promoted the "Papuanization" of the force, with Karnavian also attempting to strengthen partnerships with the government of New Zealand to implement community policing methods. In order to defuse community tensions, Karnavian personally led investigations of incidents that had the potential to trigger widespread violence—most notably, the massacre of police by Purom Wenda's OPM faction in Lanny Jaya in November 2012. Because of his example, retributive violence was not forthcoming. But individual reformers in a system that constantly rotates provincial chiefs can only have so much impact. Karnavian's successor, in fact, has shown little interest in fundamental change. Police self-financing also remains a largely unaddressed problem (Baker 2013). Unfortunately for Papua, the prospect for accelerated SSR reform during the current Joko Widodo administration is low, especially under the deeply conservative defense minister, Ryamizard Ryacudu, and the weak police chief, Badrodin Haiti. But these unsupportive circumstances notwithstanding, nonorganic troops need to be removed in synchronization with more recruitment of Papuan police. Even in the absence of broader reforms, an organic, Papuan police presence will be more welcome than migrant police, and will bring knowledge of local politics and its violent manifestations that ordinary police seem flummoxed by. By the same token, unofficial curbs on Papuan (and, for that matter, Malukan) military enrollment must be lifted.

Ending Impunity

The Enarotali incident of December 2014, in which at least four Papuans were killed by security forces, serves as a barometer for Papua's atmosphere of impunity. Indonesia's security actors have occasionally showed themselves capable of policing their own when they sell weapons to OPM (*Antara* 2015), but have been reluctant to punish their members over cases that involve the killing of Papuan civilians. As a first step to rectify this situation, civilian courts must be given jurisdiction over crimes committed by the TNI when they concern abuses toward civilians. A bill reforming the military judiciary and handing civilian courts more power over active armed forces personnel had been deliberated by parliament between 2004 and 2009, but it was ultimately aborted in the face of strong TNI resistance. Reviving this initiative might aggravate tensions between the military and the police (which would be in charge of handling TNI suspects), but this is a small price to pay for ending military impunity. Obviously, the police would also have to ensure that its own members are tried without privileges in Indonesia's civilian courts.

Investigations should begin, not end, with Enarotali. Law enforcement agencies need to investigate many more past cases. One of the most prominent cases in this regard is that of Aristoteles Masoka.

Masoka was the driver of Theys Eluay, the former independence leader who was strangled to death by Kopassus soldiers in November 2001 after attending a ceremony in the local Kopassus barracks. While Masoka went "missing," it is widely assumed that he was killed by Kopassus as well. No government official has ever mentioned Masoka's case, no investigation has ever occurred, no crime ever acknowledged. For Papuans, therefore, the impunity surrounding Masoka's fate is a symbol of how little the state values them. Investigating the case, questioning the Kopassus soldiers involved in Theys's murder, and bringing those responsible for Masoka's death to a civilian court might be the first step in building trust—not just between Jakarta and Papua, but between Jakarta and ordinary Indonesians who continue to be exposed to a culture of state violence, against which they have little protection and no redress.

Developing Papua for Papuans

Special autonomy was given to Papua in 2001 with no detailed administrative framework to guide it. In 2013 and 2014, Papua provincial Governor Lukas Enembe proposed to enhance special autonomy through "special autonomy–plus." However, rather than provide the needed framework, the draft law mainly focused on increasing the amount of funds reverting to the provinces, and the amount of discretionary spending at the governor's disposal. In proposed revisions to Enembe's draft, Agus Sumule—an advisor to Papua Barat Governor Abraham Atururi—went a long way to providing the needed framework, covering allocations for health, education, livelihoods,

> *While decentralization is often the solution to governance problems, Papua would benefit from re-centralizing government services*

and affirmative action (IPAC 2014). But these revisions were rejected by Enembe, who submitted his unrevised draft to the Ministry of Home Affairs. While then President Yudhoyono promised to take a serious look at the draft, it was clear that there was no time to get a new special autonomy law through parliament before he left office. Hence, the task of revising the 2001 law has fallen to his successor, Joko Widodo.

Papua's lack of development remains the responsibility of the national-level government. While further decentralization is often seen as the solution to many governance problems, in Papua, it appears necessary to re-centralize the management of some government services—without raising accusations of marginalizing Papuans from handling their own affairs. In this context, a coordinating ministry for Papua could be given authority for a wide variety of national, provincial, and district-level services. What would separate this ministry from previous national-level efforts in Papua, such as the failed UP4B, is the increased institutional authority entrusted to it. Ideally, the ministry would be staffed with a mix of Papuan and other Indonesian technocrats, with an adequate incentive structure and pay scale to attract capable candidates, and preference given to candidates who reside in Papua or who have meaningful field development experience in Papua.

This proposed Papua ministry would have a number of key tasks. First, it should oversee the re-centralization of health, education, and other services from the district level to Papua's two provinces. A new national-level law on regional governance (Regulation 23/2014) invests provinces with the ability to sanction district heads for failing services and, if no improvements are made, dismiss them (Pemerintah Indonesia UU23/24, Pasal 68). This law provides an implicit recognition of the damage done by decentralization, mainly through the splitting of territories. In Papua especially, many pre-existing districts—and the vast majority of new districts—are incapable of managing basic services. The re-centralized management of services at the provincial level, under the supervision of a Papua ministry, would include a competence review of every health and education civil servant. Obviously, absentee civil servants cannot simply be fired; even if they wanted to do their jobs, they have thus far not enjoyed the support structure to carry them out, and the mass termination of corrupt or absent staff would lead to social volatility, especially in the highlands. Therefore, civil servants and other public service staff should be provided with adequate training and support, in a system that provides both reward and punishment. Importantly, the government also must legitimize and fund the foundations, civil society organizations, and individuals providing health and education services in areas where the government is not. For example, Papua is distinguished by volunteers, who are present where paid teachers are absent. These individuals and institutions need recognition and formalization to bridge the period between the present failed system and a reformed mechanism in the future.

The second focus of a Papua ministry should be to further develop and enforce provincial migration policy. Papua Barat's draft for a special autonomy–plus law might serve as the basis for such a policy—namely, restricting migration of non-Papuans, monitoring entry points, and classifying migrants as temporary visitors or "seasonal workers" (IPAC 2013).

Third, the suggested ministry must advance new economic approaches that benefit the Papuan economy and native Papuans in particular. To that end, the ministry should create incentive structures for businesses that would encourage the hiring and training of indigenous workers. There should also be a special native business development tax for mining and other large companies, the proceeds from which would be used to pay for indigenous job training programs and start-up loans for indigenous businesses. Finally, the government should declare a moratorium on the establishment of new territories. This policy would be beneficial for the entire archipelago, but it is absolutely necessary for Papua if the region wants to prevent a further decline of state capacity and public services.

A Probable Future

There are few indications that the administration of Joko Widodo, inaugurated in October 2014, is prepared to adopt a fresh approach to the management of Papua. While Widodo granted clemency to five Papuan political prisoners during a visit to Papua in April 2015, many of the government's other policies resemble the failed Papua strategy of the administration of Megawati Sukarnoputri, to whose party Widodo belongs. For example, Home Affairs Minister Tjaho Kumalo announced in April 2015 that more Papuan provinces will be created (*Republika* 2014). Similarly, Minister for Village Development, Disadvantaged Regions and Transmigration Marwan Jafar suggested that transmigration will begin again, because Papua has so much "empty land." In addition, the security for Javanese migrants would be provided by the military (*Detik News* 2014). A new military command, Kodam XVIII/Kasuari, has been proposed for Papua

Barat. And despite much outcry from highland civil society and churches, as well as the local parliament, a new mobile police brigade base is planned for Jayawijaya (Liputan 6, 2015).

The continuation of the current policy paradigm—ongoing in-migration, more administrative splits, poor health and education services—may over time reduce the ability of Papuans to resist, but it won't address the source of discontent, disillusionment, and even hatred toward Jakarta among many citizens of the territory. But alternative pathways are possible, both for Jakarta and Papua. Jakarta could rethink its traditional policies and begin to seriously focus on public service delivery and the socioeconomic emancipation of indigenous Papuans, while Papuans may move toward a transcending of clan identity and leadership. The urgent need for this latter move is being heard in the KINGMI and GIDI congregations, giving them a potential role in future negotiations between Papua and the center. The churches are not implicated in corruption or clan politics, and although they have a mainly highland constituency, they appeal to the lowlands as well. A combination of consolidated leadership, emphasis on unity, and tactics such as civil disobedience will certainly pay more dividends than an insurgency, which will pay out fear and death.

However, it is also important to note that further escalation remains a dangerously probable scenario. Papuan frustration may yet foment into a new insurgency, and the scattered OPM units could be sidelined by an entity that is able to raise funds and access quality weapons. It takes little imagination to picture an armed wing forming within the KNPB. In fact, the militancy and frustration within its membership provide fertile ground for such a develop-

> *An armed resistance similar to that in Aceh in the 1980s, 1990s, and early 2000s is not unthinkable*

ment. For Indonesia, the struggle of the OPM is still a distant insurrection, but a transformation into an armed resistance similar to that in Aceh in the 1980s, 1990s, and early 2000s is not unthinkable. The government has yet to understand that it has been lucky thus far that the OPM is so disorganized and disparate. Jakarta must take steps now because the future, without redress, will be untenable—and it may also be bloody.

Endnotes

1. In addition to Scott (2009), this paper draws from Joel S. Migdal's analytical frameworks, particularly those articulated in *State in Society* (2004). Migdal discards the restrictive "Weberian" definition of the state, recognizing that Weber posited an ideal state in which every state is only measured by its distance from the ideal. Migdal's framework recognizes the diverse actors who may reshape state practices and policies to fit local norms.

2. The latest "prophetary" incident of note in Papua involved the seizure of a remote airstrip in Kapeso, Mamberamo Tengah, in June 2009. A Christian sect led by an ex-soldier believed that their revolt and runway seizure would herald the return of the Messiah (*Jakarta Post* 2009).

3. Catholicism proved popular in Papua's south, while indigenous converts to Islam were found on the western coast and islands—a legacy of small-scale trade in slaves between that coast and the sultanates of Ternate and Tidore.

4. In between the New York Agreement and the Act of Free Choice, Suharto deposed Sukarno and destroyed the Indonesian Communist Party (PKI), killing somewhere between five hundred thousand and two million Indonesians in the process.

5. This observation is based upon the author's travels on the Indonesian border with PNG, particularly in Keerom, Merauke, and Boven Digoel. Also see Manning and Rumbiak (1987).

6. The author has heard of such collaboration in Wamena, Pyramid, Eragayem, Binime, Bokondini, and other areas—so many that the stories point to patterns of cooperation rather than isolated incidents.

7. On July 6, 1998, the Indonesian military shot dead numerous protesters who had coalesced around a *Bintang Kejora* raised by civil servant Filep Karma on Biak Island in Cenderawasih Bay; the military also apparently killed detainees at a later time and dumped their bodies at sea.

8. As of February 2015, 38 Papuan detainees are in jail for political offenses (Papuans Behind Bars, http://www.papuansbehindbars.org).

9. Hendropriyono was instrumental in the creation of Papua Barat. Ryacudu, for his part, publicly declared that Theys Eluay's murderers were heroes.

10. Interview with an Indonesian doctor working in Jayapura, April 2014.

11. Interviews with Dinas Kesehatan Jayawijaya and Yahukimo staff, as well as local church foundation workers, November 2012.

12. Interview with GIDI church health clinic staff, Wamena, March 2015.

13. ViCIS and SNPK data are available online: http://www.snpk-indonesia.com.

14. A more accurate measurement of violence in Papua could likely only occur through church sources. However, such data collection and analysis would be complicated by the sheer number of denominations, as well as their propensity to withhold the demographic information they collect. They are often the only entities recording births and deaths in rural areas.

15. For the radio documentary, see http://www.abc.net.au/radionational/programs/360/eat-pray-mourn/4598026.

16. Unlike the ViCIS study, the newer SNPK data contains a specific "separatist" category distinct from political violence, but does not disaggregate the particular identity of a victim either.

17. Bambang Darmono, speaking at an UP4B meeting with international donors on February 2, 2012.

18. This figure breaks down into 11,000 TNI Army (*Angkatan Darurat*); 1,272 TNI Marines (*Mariner*); and 57 TNI Air Force (*Angkatan Udara*).

19. Nonorganic forces are relocated from their permanent duty stations to areas of unrest, whereas organic forces reside in permanent duty stations.

20. Interviews with church workers and two TNI privates, Tolikara and Yahukimo, September 2012.

21. Conversations with soldiers smuggling gold from Intan Jaya (Nabire, October 2013) and soldiers involved in gold-mining operations on Buru Island, Maluku (November 2013).

22. Community focus group discussions and interviews with teachers and church workers, Tolikara and Yahukimo, 2012–13.

23. Interviews with community members, including primary school teachers and a private-school principal, Bokondini, 2013.

24. This description of intelligence activities has been collated from the author's discussions with journalists, rights activists, police, embassy staff, and military attachés, conducted from 2010 to 2015. Among them were police intelligence officials in Jayapura and Wamena, and a BIN representative in Jakarta.

25. Interviews with Jakarta-based political affairs officers from two Western embassies that conducted frequent visits to Papua, Jayapura, 2013.

26. See, for example, the speech of Strategic Reserve (Kostrad) Commander Lieutenant General Gatot Nurmantyo to college students at the Bandung Institute of Technology on May 2, 2014, where he discussed separatism as part of a proxy war waged against Indonesia by foreign interests: http://www.uny.ac.id/berita/peran-pemuda-dalam-menghadapi-proxy-war.html (accessed April 11, 2015). Nurmantyo continued to espouse his proxy war theories as army chief of staff (IPAC 2015). In July of 2015 he was appointed head of the Indonesian military by President Widodo.

27. A new concerning trend is the use of special autonomy funding by local governments to pay compensation to victims of such conflicts. This has resulted in clan "wars" that may not have begun were it not for the "value" of the wounded and dead.

28. Interview with local church workers, Tolikara, August 2011.

29. Interviews in Nalca with a local clan leader and volunteer teachers in a church, Yayasan, 2011–2013.

30. The bulk of the jade trade, however, is under *Tatmadaw* control (*NYT* 2014).

31. By the time of the CPB's disintegration, the party's rank and file was constituted mainly of ethnic Wa (Lintner and Black 2009). The UWSP eventually shifted from heroin to methamphetamine; at present, they are one of the biggest methamphetamine producers in Southeast Asia (ibid).

32. The clearly exaggerated (read: manipulated) population increases in newly created districts suggest that there are significantly fewer indigenous persons than current statistics indicate, especially in the highlands.

33. According to highland health care workers interviewed by the author, Papuan birth rates have been declining. Church elders have also noted declining birth registrations over the last 20 years. While various explanations have been offered, the author knows of no study that has systematically sought to uncover why this is occurring.

34. The author uses an average 2010 exchange rate of 9,086.05 IDR = 1 USD.

35. The 2010 GDRP in Papua province was 87,733 trillion rupiah, while in Papua Barat it was 26,873 trillion. The 2010 BPS figures are the latest relatively accurate ones; the 2011 and 2012 statistics are available, but the former are referred to as "preliminary," while the latter are "very preliminary."

36. Personal communication with numerous former and current Amnesty International staff, including IPAC Director Sidney Jones, who worked in Amnesty International (UK) in the 1980s.

37. The Yale report overwhelmingly references only two works: the TAPOL report and Osborne (1985). This is the same report referred to as a "warning" by Robinson (2012).

38. A majority of Papuans who are aware of HIV/AIDS believe that the government of Indonesia purposefully introduced it. This was asserted to the author countless times from 2010 to the present.

39. Details of this case are found in Bachelard (2013).

40. For example: the April 29, 2015, demonstration demanding "open access to West Papua" by the Free West Papua Campaign (UK). See http://freewestpapua.org/2015/04/01/london-demonstration-open-access-to-west-papua/, accessed April 12, 2015.

41. These restrictions are lessening. Fairfax Media correspondent Michael Bachelard has been granted two recent visits to Papua: his first story (Bachelard 2013) was hardly flattering to the government, but this did not stop the government from granting him permission for a second trip. Mark Davis, a correspondent with the Australian network SBS, was also allowed to enter Papua (Davis 2014). On May 10, 2015, President Joko Widodo announced that all restrictions on the foreign press have been "lifted," but it remains to be seen if this will actually occur (*Jakarta Post* 2015).

42. Personal communications with PBI staff and a member of the PBI international secretariat, October–November 2010.

43. The network consultations and meetings that occurred prior to the announcement did not include discussions related to that recommendation; nearly all the network participants were blindsided by this. These observations were expressed to the author in personal conversations with Papua Peace Network participants and LIPI researchers in Jayapura, October–November 2011.

Bibliography

Amnesty International. 2012. "Indonesia: Investigate Military Attacks on Villagers in Wamena, Papua," June 8. [https://www.amnesty.org/en/documents/ASA21/020/2012/en/, accessed October 13, 2014].

Anderson, Bobby. 2013a. "Living without a State," *Inside Indonesia* 110. [http://insideindonesia.org/living-without-a-state, accessed November 1, 2014].

———. 2013b. "The Failure of Education in the Papuan Highlands," *Inside Indonesia* 113. [http://www.insideindonesia.org/the-failure-of-education-in-papua-s-highlands, accessed November 1, 2014].

———. 2013c. "Gangster, Ideologue, Martyr: The Posthumous Reinvention of Teungku Badruddin and the Nature of the Free Aceh Movement." *Conflict, Security & Development* 13 (1): 31–56.

———. 2014a. "Dying for Nothing," *Inside Indonesia* 115. [http://www.insideindonesia.org/dying-for-nothing, accessed November 1, 2014].

———. 2014b. "Platitudes of Papua," *Inside Indonesia* 115. [http://www.insideindonesia.org/platitudes-of-papua, accessed November 1, 2014].

———. 2014c. "Famine and Fraud," *Inside Indonesia* 117. [http://www.insideindonesia.org/famine-and-fraud, accessed November 1, 2014].

———. 2014d. "Bemused Spectators and Political Animals at the Tolikara Trough," *New Mandala*, April 4. [http://asiapacific.anu.edu.au/newmandala/2014/04/04/bemused-spectators-and-political-animals-at-the-tolikara-trough/, accessed March 2, 2014].

Antara News. 2015. "Oknum TNI Jual Amunisi, Nyawa Semakin Mudah Melayang," January 29. [http://papua.antaranews.com/berita/448902/oknum-tni-jual-amunisi-nyawa-semakin-mudah-melayang, accessed April 12, 2015].

Arios, Rois Leonard. 2012. "Tindak Kekerasan pada Konflik Pilkada: Sebuah Analisis Teori Konstruksi Sosial," *Kompasiana*, March 18. [http://sosbud.kompa-siana.com/2012/03/18/tindak-kekerasan-pada-konflik-pilkada-sebuah-analisis-teori-konstruksi-sosial-443167.html, accessed December 10, 2014].

Asian Human Rights Commission. 2013. *The Neglected Genocide: Human Rights Abuses against Papuans in the Central Highlands, 1977–1978*. [http://www.humanrightspapua.org, accessed May 10, 2014].

Aspinall, Edward. 2006. *Selective Outrage and Unacknowledged Fantasies: Rethinking Papua, Indonesia and Australia*. Nautilus Institute for Security and Sustainability, Austral Policy Forum. [http://www.nautilus.org/~rmit/forum-reports/0615a-aspinall.html, accessed May 4, 2014].

———. 2009. "Combatants to Contractors." *Indonesia* 87, April: 1-34.

Australian Broadcasting Corporation. 2006. *Light Night Live*, Radio National, April 28.

———. 2012. "Rare Look Inside Papua Independence Movement," Australian Broadcasting Corporation, August 27. [http://www.abc.net.au/7.30/content/2012/s3577104.htm, accessed June 21, 2014].

Australian Agency for International Development. 2006. *Impacts of HIV/AIDS 2005–2025 in Papua New Guinea, Indonesia and East Timor*. Canberra: AusAID.

Bachelard, Michael. 2013. "They're Taking Our Children," *Sydney Morning Herald*, April 29. [http://www.smh.com.au/lifestyle/theyre-taking-our-children-20130503-2inhf.html, accessed April 11, 2015].

———. 2015. "High Tension in Papua and West Papua," *Sydney Morning Herald*, February 7. [http://www.smh.com.au/good-weekend/high-tension-in-papua-and-west-papua-20150206-12uc2d.html, accessed April 11, 2015].

Badan Pusat Statistik. 2010. *Indonesia Census 2010*. Jakarta: BPS.

———. 2012. *Indonesia Demographic and Health Survey (IDHS)*. Jakarta: BPS.

———. 2013. Select poverty measurements and indicators by province. Jakarta: BPS. [http://www.bps.go.id/, accessed May 15, 2015.]

Baker, Jacqui. 2013. "The Parman Economy: Post-Authoritarian Shifts in the Off-Budget Economy of Indonesia's Security Institutions." *Indonesia* 96: 123–150.

Bell, Ian, Herb Feith, and Ron Hatley. 1986. "The West Papuan Challenge to Indonesian Authority in Irian Jaya: Old Problems, New Possibilities." *Asian Survey* 26 (5): 539–556.

Bintang Papua. 2014. "Anggota DPRD Tolikara Dikeroyok Hingga Tewas," January 30. [http://bintangpapua.com/index.php/2012-12-03-03-14-02/kenambayumbay/item/990-anggota-dprd-tolikara-dikeroyok-hingga-tewas, accessed January 04, 2015].

Bone, Robert C. 1958. *The Dynamics of the Western New Guinea Problem.* Interim report from the Modern Indonesian Project, Southeast Asia Program, Dept. of Far Eastern Studies, Cornell University.

Brundige, Elizabeth, Winter King, Priyneha Vahali, Stephen Vladeck, and Xiang Yuan. 2004. *Indonesian Human Rights Abuses in West Papua: Application of the Law of Genocide to the History of Indonesian Control.* Allard K. Lowenstein International Human Rights Clinic, Yale Law School. [http://www.law. yale.edu/documents/pdf/Intellectual_Life/West_Papua_final_report.pdf, accessed June 2, 2014].

Chasie, Charles, and Sanjoy Hazarika. 2009. *The State Strikes Back: India and the Naga Insurgency.* Policy Studies 52. Washington, DC: East-West Center Washington.

Chauvel, Richard. 2005a. *Constructing Papuan Nationalism: History, Ethnicity, and Adaptation.* Policy Studies 14. Washington, DC: East-West Center Washington.

————. 2005b. *Papuan Political Imaginings of the 1960s: International Conflict and Local Nationalisms.* Seminar on the Act of Free Choice, Den Haag, Netherlands, November 15. [http://resources.huygens.knaw.nl/indonesischebetrekkingen1945-1969/DekolonisatieVanIndonesieEnHetZelfbeschikkingsrechtVanDePapoea/papers_pdf/chauvel, accessed June 21, 2015].

Chauvel, Richard, and Ikrar Nusa Bhakti. 2004. *The Papua Conflict: Jakarta's Perceptions and Policies.* Policy Studies 5. Washington, DC: East-West Center Washington.

Conboy, Kenneth J. 2004. *Intel: Inside Indonesia's Intelligence Service.* Jakarta: Equinox Publishing.

Cribb, Robert. 2001. "How Many Deaths? Problems in the Statistics of Massacre in Indonesia (1965–1966) and East Timor (1975–1980)." In Ingrid Wessel and Georgia Wimhöfer, eds. 2001. *Violence in Indonesia.* Hamburg: Abera.

Darroch, George P. 2009. *Portraying Papua: Activist Representations of Indonesian Papua, 1969–2009.* MPhil thesis, Australian National University.

Davis, Mark. 2014. "West Papua's New Dawn?" SBS Television, June 3. [http://www. sbs.com.au/news/dateline/story/west-papuas-new-dawn, accessed April 11, 2015].

Dean, Karin. 2012. "Struggle Over Space in Myanmar: Expanding State Territoriality after the Kachin Ceasefire." In Miller, Michelle Ann, ed. *Autonomy and Armed Separatism in South and Southeast Asia.* 2012. Singapore: Institute of Southeast Asian Studies, 113–135.

Detik News. 2014. "Menteri Marwan Ingin Buat Orang Jawa Tertarik Transmigrasi ke Papua," October 30. [http://news.detik.com/read/2014/10/30/123039/2734296/10/menteri-marwan-ingin-buat-orang-jawa-tertarik-transmigrasi-ke-papua, accessed October 30, 2014].

Dinas Pendidikan Propinsi Papua. 2011. *Rencana Pembangunan Pendidikan Dasar dan Menengah Propinsi Papua.* Jayapura: Dinas Pendidikan Propinsi Papua.

Drooglever, Pieter. 2010. *An Act of Free Choice: Decolonisation and the Right to Self-Determination in West Papua.* Oxford: Oneworld Publications.

Elmslie, Jim. 2003. *Irian Jaya Under the Gun.* Honolulu: University of Hawai'i Press.

———. 2010. *West Papuan Demographic Transition and the 2010 Indonesian Census: "Slow Motion Genocide" or Not?* University of Sydney, CPACS Working Paper No. 11/1, September.

Elmslie, Jim, and Camellia Webb-Gannon. 2013. "A Slow Motion Genocide: Indonesian Rule in West Papua." *Griffith Journal of Law and Human Dignity*, 1 (2): 142–166.

Elmslie, Jim, and Camellia Webb-Gannon with Peter King. 2011. *Anatomy of an Occupation: The Indonesian Military in West Papua.* Sydney: Centre for Peace and Conflict Studies, University of Sydney.

Farhadian, Charles. 2005. *Christianity, Islam and Nationalism in Indonesia.* London: Routledge.

Farmer, Paul. 2003. *Pathologies of Power: Health, Human Rights, and the New War on the Poor.* Berkeley: University of California Press.

French, Patrick. 2003. *Tibet, Tibet: A Personal History of a Lost Land.* New York: Knopf.

Galtung, Johann. 1969. "Violence, Peace, and Peace Research." *Journal of Peace Research* 6 (3): 167–191.

Government of Indonesia. 2014. *Undang-Undang Republik Indonesia Nomor 23 Tahun 2014 Tentang Pemerintah Daerah.* [http://www.kemendagri.go.id/media/documents/2014/10/15/u/u/uu_23_tahun_2014.pdf, accessed May 25, 2015.]

Griffiths, Jay. 2011. "Songs and Freedom in West Papua," *The Guardian*, March 15.

Harsono, Andreas. 2007. "Global Integrity Report 2006," posted October 1. [http://www.andreasharsono.net/2007/10/global-integrity-report-2006.html, accessed April 12, 2015].

Herald Sun. 2011. "An Act of Free Choice, But Hugh Saw the Guns," December 19. [http://www.heraldsun.com.au/news/opinion/a-free-choice-but-hugh-saw-the-guns/story-e6frfhqf-1226225266257, accessed April 11, 2015].

Herawati, Titi. 1998. *Studi Pengembangan Pemukiman untuk Alokasi Penempatan Penduduk Daerah Transmigrasi (APPDT).* Jakarta: Pusat Penelitian dan pengembangan, Departemen Transmigrasi dan Pemukiman Perambah Hutan.

Hernawan, Yohanes Budi. 2013. *From the Theatre of Torture to the Theatre of Peace: The Politics of Torture and Re-imagining Peacebuilding in Papua, Indonesia.* PhD thesis, Australian National University.

Human Rights Watch. 2006. *Too High a Price: The Human Rights Cost of the Indonesian Military's Economic Activities.* HRW Report 18/5(C). [http://www.hrw.org/reports/2006/indonesia0606/indonesia0606web.pdf, accessed April 12, 2015].

———. 2007. *Out of Sight: Endemic Abuse and Impunity in Papua's Central Highlands.* HRW Report 19/10(C). [http://www.hrw.org/reports/2007/papua0707/papua0707web.pdf, accessed July 8, 2014].

———. 2011. "Indonesia: Independent Investigation Needed into Papua Violence," posted October 28. [http://www.hrw.org/news/2011/10/28/indonesia-independent-investigation-needed-papua-violence, accessed February 2, 2014].

Hyslop, Leah. 2011. "Benny Wenda: 'There's a Silent Genocide Going on in West Papua,'" *Daily Telegraph*, November 28. [http://www.telegraph.co.uk/expat/expatlife/8920491/Benny-Wenda-Theres-a-silent-genocide-going-on-in-West-Papua.html, accessed May 25, 2015].

Indonesian Institute of Sciences. 2008. *Papua Road Map.* [http://sydney.edu.au/arts/peace_conflict/docs/PAPUA_ROAD_MAP_Short_Eng.pdf, accessed August 5, 2014].

Institute for Policy Analysis of Conflict. 2013. *Carving Up Papua: More Districts, More Trouble.* IPAC Report 3, October 9. [http://file.understandingconflict.org/file/2013/10/IPAC_Carving_Up_Papua_More_Districts_More_Problems.pdf, accessed August 1, 2014].

———. 2014. *Papua Update: The Latest on Otsus Plus.* IPAC Report 7, February 27. [http://file.understandingconflict.org/file/2014/02/IPAC_No7_Latest_on_Otsus_Plus.pdf, accessed April 11, 2015].

———. 2015. *The Expanding Role of the Indonesian Military.* IPAC Report 19, May 25. [http://file.understandingconflict.org/file/2015/05/IPAC_19_Expanding_Role_of_TNI.pdf, accessed July 4, 2015.]

International Crisis Group. 2003. *Dividing Papua: How Not to Do It.* Asia Briefing 24, April 9. [http://www.crisisgroup.org/~/media/Files/asia/south-east-asia/indonesia/B Dividing Papua How Not To Do It.pdf, accessed July 22, 2014].

———. 2006. *Papua: Answers to Frequently Asked Questions.* Asia Briefing 53, September 5.

———. 2010a. *Radicalisation and Dialogue in Papua.* Asia Report 188, March 11. [http://www.crisisgroup.org/~/media/Files/asia/south-east-asia/indonesia/188_radicalisation_and_dialogue_in_papua.pdf, accessed August 1, 2014].

———. 2011. *Indonesia: Hope and Hard Reality in Papua.* Asia Briefing 126, August 22. [http://www.crisisgroup.org/~/media/Files/asia/south-east-asia/indonesia/B126 Papua - Hope and Hard Reality.pdf, accessed August 1, 2014].

———. 2012. *Indonesia: Dynamics of Violence in Papua.* Asia Report 232, August 9. [http://www.crisisgroup.org/~/media/Files/asia/south-east-asia/indonesia/232-indonesia-dynamics-of-violence-in-papua.pdf, accessed August 4, 2014].

Irawaddy. 2013. "Shan Group Accuses Kachin Rebels of Rights Abuses," October 31. [http://www.irrawaddy.org/latest-news/shan-group-accuses-kachin-rebels-rights-abuses.html, accessed January 1, 2015].

Jakarta Globe. 2011. "Low-ranking Soldiers Indicted Over Torture Killing in Puncak Jaya," July 22. [http://www.thejakartaglobe.com/archive/low-ranking-soldiers-indicted-over-torture-killing-in-papuas-puncak-jaya, accessed October 30, 2014].

Jakarta Post. 2009. "Police Retake Airstrip from 'TNI Deserter'-led Group," June 8. [http://www.thejakartapost.com/news/2009/06/08/police-retake-airstrip-tni-deserter039led-group.html, accessed January 6, 2014].

———. 2014. "60 Brimob Personnel Withdrawn from Lanny Jaya," October 6. [http://www.thejakartapost.com/news/2014/10/16/60-brimob-personnel-withdrawn-lanny-jaya.html, accessed December 2, 2014].

———. 2015. "Foreign Journalists Now 'Free' to Report on Papua, Says Jokowi," May 10. [http://www.thejakartapost.com/news/2015/05/10/foreign-journalists-now-free-report-papua-says-jokowi.html, accessed May 25, 2015].

Jianxiong Ma. 2013. *The Lahu Minority in Southwest China: A Response to Ethnic Marginalization on the Frontier.* London: Routledge.

JUBI. 2011. "DAP: Papua on the Brink of Genocide," *Tabloid Jubi,* Jayapura, March 4.

Karnavian, Tito. 2014. *Bhayangkara di Bumi Cendrawasih.* Jakarta: Indonesia Strategic Policy Institute.

Kementrian Kesehatan Republik Indonesia. 2012. *Profil Kesehatan Indonesia.* Jakarta: Kementerian Kesehatan RI.

King, Peter. 2004. *West Papua and Indonesia Since Suharto: Independence, Autonomy or Chaos?* Sydney: University of New South Wales Press.

———. 2006. "In Defence of the Papua Sympathisers: A Rejoinder to Ed Aspinall." *Policy and Society*, 25 (4): 131–137.

Kirksey, Eben. 2012. *Freedom in Entangled Worlds: West Papua and the Architecture of Global Power*. Durham: Duke University Press.

Kirksey, Eben, and Andreas Harsono. 2007. "Criminal Collaborations? Antonius Wamang and the Indonesian Military in Timika." *South East Asia Research* 16 (2): 165–197.

Kivimaki, Timo, and Ruben Thorning. 2002. "Democratization and Regional Power Sharing in Papua/Irian Jaya: Increased Opportunities and Decreased Motivations for Violence." *Asian Survey* 42 (4).

Kontras (Komisi Untuk Orang Hilang dan Korban Tindak Kekerasan). 2014. "Penembakan dan Pembunuhan Sewenang – Wenang di Enarotali, Paniai; Segera Bentuk Tim Independen, Pulihkan Korban dan Masyarakat," December 9. [http://www.kontras.org/index.php?hal=siaran_pers&id=1979, accessed May 2, 2015].

Kumar Das, Samir. 2007. *Conflict and Peace in India's Northeast: The Role of Civil Society*. Policy Studies 42. Washington, DC: East-West Center Washington.

Leach, Edmund. 1954. *Political Systems of Highland Burma: A Study of Kachin Social Structure*. London: Athlone Press.

Leadbeater, Maire. 2005. "On the Brink of Genocide," *New Zealand Herald*, November 16.

Leith, Denise. 2003. *The Politics of Power: Freeport in Suharto's Indonesia*. Honolulu: University of Hawai'i Press.

Lintner, Bertil. 1990. *The Rise and Fall of the Communist Party of Burma (CPB)*. Ithaca, New York: Cornell University Southeast Asia Program.

———. 1997. *The Kachin: Lords of Burma's Northern Frontier*. Chiang Mai: Asia Film House.

———. 2011. *Land of Jade: A Journey from India through Northern Burma to China*. Bangkok: Orchard Press.

Lintner, Bertil, and Michael Black. 2009. *Merchants of Madness: The Methamphetamine Explosion in the Golden Triangle*. Chiang Mai: Silkworm Books.

Liputan 6. 2015. "DPR Papua Tolak Pembangunan Mako Brimob di Wamena," January 28. [http://news.liputan6.com/read/2167349/dpr-papua-tolak-pembangunan-mako-brimob-di-wamena, accessed April 12, 2015].

MacLeod, Jason. 2010. "Papuan Struggle Enters New Phase," *Open Democracy*, July 26. [https://www.opendemocracy.net/jason-macleod/papuan-struggle-enters-new-phase, accessed April 11, 2015].

Manning, Chris, and Michael Rumbiak. 1987. "Irian Jaya: Economic Change, Migrant Labour and Indigenous Welfare." In Hill, Hall, ed. 1989. *Unity and Diversity: Regional Economic Development in Indonesia Since 1970*. Oxford: Oxford University Press.

Marshall, A.J., and B.M. Beehler. 2007. *The Ecology of Papua* (Ecology of Indonesia Series). Hong Kong: Periplus.

May, Brian. 1978. *The Indonesian Tragedy*. Singapore: Routledge.

McGibbon, Rodd. 2004. *Plural Society in Peril: Migration, Economic Change, and the Papua Conflict*. Policy Studies 13. Washington, DC: East-West Center Washington.

———. 2006. *Pitfalls of Papua: Understanding the Conflict and Its Place in Australia-Indonesia Relations*. Lowy Institute Paper 13. Canberra: Lowry Institute for International Policy.

Mietzner, Marcus. 2006. *The Politics of Military Reform in Post-Suharto Indonesia: Elite Conflict, Nationalism, and Institutional Resistance*. Policy Studies 23. Washington, DC: East-West Center Washington.

———. 2009. "Autonomy, Democracy, and Internal Conflict: The 2006 Gubernatorial Elections in Papua." In Erb, Maribeth, and Priyambudi Sulistiynto, eds. 2009. *Deepening Democracy in Indonesia? Direct Elections for Local Leaders*. Singapore: ISEAS.

———. 2011. "The Political Marginalization of the Military in Indonesia." In Mietzner, Marcus, ed. *The Political Resurgence of the Military in Southeast Asia: Conflict and Leadership*. New York: Routledge, 127–147.

Mietzner, Marcus, and Lisa Misol. 2012. "Military Businesses in Post-Suharto Indonesia: Decline, Reform and Persistence." In Rüland, Jürgen, Maria-Gabriela Manea, and Hans Born, eds. 2013. *The Politics of Military Reform: Experiences from Indonesia and Nigeria*. New York: Springer.

Migdal, Joel S. 2004. *State in Society: Studying How States and Societies Transform and Constitute One Another*. Cambridge: Cambridge University Press.

Monbiot, George. 1989. *Poisoned Arrows: An Investigative Journey through Indonesia*. London: Macmillan.

National Violence Monitoring System (Sistem Nasional Pemantauan Kekerasan or SNPK, previously the Violent Conflict in Indonesia Study or ViCIS).

Government of Indonesia, Coordinating Ministry for Human Development and Culture. [http://www.snpk-indonesia.com, accessd on June 21, 2015.]

New York Times. 2014. "Searching for Burmese Jade, and Finding Misery," December 1. [http://www.nytimes.com/2014/12/02/world/searching-for-burmese-jade-and-finding-misery.html, accessed May 22, 2015.]

Osborne, Robin. 1985. *Indonesia's Secret War: The Guerilla Struggle in Irian Jaya*. Sydney: Allen and Unwin.

Perwira, Ita. 2014. *Women's Access to Health Services in the Highlands of Papua*. A Report Commissioned by the World Bank Indonesia–PNPM Support Facility.

Premdas, Ralph P. 1985. "The Organisasi Papua Merdeka in Irian Jaya: Continuity and change in Papua New Guinea's relations with Indonesia." *Asian Survey* 25 (10); 1055–1074.

Rajagopalan, Swarna. 2008. *Peace Accords in Northeast India: Journey over Milestones*. Policy Studies 46. Washington, DC: East-West Center Washington.

Rees, Susan J., Remco van de Pas, Derrick Silove, and Moses Kareth. 2008. "Health and Human Security in West Papua." *Medical Journal of Australia* 189: 641–643.

Republika. 2014. "Mendagri Prioritaskan Pemekaran Dua Provinsi di Papua," October 31. [http://m.republika.co.id/berita/nasional/umum/14/10/31/neanre-mendagri-prioritaskan-pemekaran-dua-provinsi-di-papua, accessed April 12, 2015].

Robinson, Jennifer. 2012. "The UN's Chequered Record in West Papua," *Al Jazeera Online*, March 21. [http://www.aljazeera.com/indepth/opinion/2012/03/201232172539145809.html, accessed May 25, 2015].

Rutherford, Danilyn. 2003. *Raiding the Land of the Foreigners: The Limits of the Nation on an Indonesian Frontier*. Princeton: Princeton University Press.

Sahlins, Marshall. 1963. "Poor Man, Rich Man, Big Man, Chief: Political Types in Melanesia and Polynesia." *Comparative Studies in Society and History*, 5 (3): 285–303.

Saltford, John. 2000. *UNTEA and UNRWI: United Nations Involvement in West New Guinea During the 1960's*. PhD dissertation, University of Hull.

Savage, Peter. 1978. "The Nationalist Struggle in West Irian: The Divisions Within the Liberation." *Journal of Sociology* 14 (2).

Schulze, Kristen E. 2004. *The Free Aceh Movement (GAM): Anatomy of a Separatist Organization*. Policy Studies 2. Washington, DC: East-West Center Washington.

Scott, James C. 2009. *The Art of Not Being Governed: An Anarchist History of Upland Southeast Asia*. New Haven: Yale Agrarian Studies Series.

Simpson, Bradley. 2010. *Economists with Guns: Authoritarian Development and US-Indonesia Relations, 1960–1968*. Stanford: Stanford University Press.

Singh, Chandrika. 2004. *Naga Politics: A Critical Account*. New Delhi: Mittal Publications.

Smith, Martin. 1994. *Ethnic Groups in Burma: Development, Democracy and Human Rights*. London: Anti-Slavery International.

Sosa, Naomi. 2014. *Gender Inclusion and PNPM-RESPEK in Papua's Highlands*. A Report Commissioned by the World Bank Indonesia–PNPM Support Facility.

Stott, David Adam. 2011. "Would an Independent West Papua Be a Failing State?" *Asia-Pacific Journal* 9 (37/1), September 12. [http://www.japanfocus.org/David_Adam-Stott/3597, accessed January 6, 2013].

Suara Pembaruan. 2011. "KNPB Tuntut Referendum Papua," November 14.

Sydney Morning Herald. 2010. "Video Shows Papuans Being Tortured," October 17. [http://m.smh.com.au/world/video-shows-papuans-being-tortured-20101017-16p7f.html, accessed March 27, 2013].

TAPOL. 1983. *West Papua: The Obliteration of a People*. London: TAPOL.

TAPOL. 1988. *West Papua: The Obliteration of a People*. London: TAPOL. Third edition: revised and substantially rewritten.

Taylor, Jean Gelman. 2003. *Indonesia: Peoples and Histories*. London: Yale University Press.

Timmer, Jaap. 2007a. "A Brief Social and Political History of Papua, 1962–2005." In Marshall, A. J., and B.M. Beehler, eds. 2007. *The Ecology of Papua*. Singapore: Periplus.

———. 2007b. "Erring Decentralization and Elite Politics in Papua." In Nordholt, Henk Schulte, and Gerry van Klinken, eds. 2007. *Renegotiating Boundaries: Local Politics in Post-Suharto Indonesia*. Leiden: KITLV Press.

Unger, Jonathan. 1997. "Not Quite Han: The Ethnic Minorities of China's Southwest." *Bulletin of Concerned Asian Scholars* 29 (3): 67–76.

United Nations. 1948. *Convention on the Prevention and Punishment of the Crime of Genocide*, in Resolution 260 (III), December 9.

United Nations Development Program. 1968. *A Design for Development in West Irian*.

Report prepared for the government of Indonesia by the UNDP and Fund of the United Nations for the Development of West Irian.

United States Department of State. 2013. *Indonesia Human Rights Report.* Washington, DC: US Dept. of State [http://www.state.gov/j/drl/rls/hrrpt/2013/eap/220196.htm, accessed April 11, 2015].

Upadhyay, Archana. 2009. *India's Fragile Borderlands: The Dynamics of Terrorism in Northeast India.* London: Tauris.

Upton, Stuart. 2009. *The Impact of Migration on the People of Papua, Indonesia: A Historical Demographic Analysis.* PhD dissertation, University of New South Wales.

Van der Kroef, Justus M. 1958. *The West New Guinea Dispute.* New York: Institute of Pacific Relations.

———. 1961. "Nationalism and Politics in West New Guinea." *Pacific Affairs* XXXIV (1): 38–53.

———. 1962. "Toward Papua Barat," *The Australian Quarterly*, March: 17–26.

———. 1968. "West New Guinea: The Uncertain Future." *Asian Survey* 8 (8): 691–707.

Van der Veur, Paul W. 1963. "West Irian in the Indonesian Fold." *Asian Survey* 3 (7): 334–336.

Van Klinken, Jerry. 2007. *Communal Violence and Democratization in Indonesia: Small Town Wars.* Routledge Contemporary Southeast Asia Series, No. 15.

Van Schendel, Willem. 2002. "Geographies of Knowing, Geographies of Ignorance: Jumping Scale in Southeast Asia." *Environment and Planning D: Society and Space* 20: 647–668.

Violent Conflict in Indonesia Study (ViCIS). 2010. World Bank and the Indonesian State Development Planning Board (Badan Perencanaan Pembangunan Nasional, or BAPPENAS, 2008–2011). Internal presentation to USAID, Jakarta, June 21.

Visser, Leontine. 2013. *Governing New Guinea: An Oral History of Papuan Administrators, 1950–1990.* Leiden: Brill.

Vriend, Willem Hendrik. 2003. *Smoky Fires: The Merits of Development Cooperation for the Inculturation of Health Improvements.* Unpublished thesis, Vrije Universiteit Amsterdam.

Wanandi, Jusuf. 2012. *Shades of Grey: A Political Memoir of Modern Indonesia, 1965–1998.* Jakarta: Equinox.

Welsh, Bridget. 2008. "Local and National: Keroyokan Mobbing in Indonesia." *Journal of East Asian Studies* 8 (3): 473–504.

Wenda, Benny. 2013. "West Papua: Things Are Not Getting 'Better' for Us," *The Guardian*, October 11. [http://www.theguardian.com/commentisfree/2013/oct/11/west-papua-tony-abbott-australia, accessed on May 23, 2015].

Wing, John, and Peter King. 2005. *Genocide in West Papua? The Role of the Indonesian State Apparatus and a Current Needs Assessment of the Papuan People.* Sydney: CPACS, University of Sydney.

World Bank. 1988. *Indonesia: The Transmigration Program in Perspective.* Washington, DC: The World Bank.

YouTube. 2010. "Indonesian Police/BRIMOB Officers Tour Tourte and Kill of Yawan Wayeni.[sic]" [https://www.youtube.com/watch?v=FfovSnOTLZo, accessed April 11, 2015].

———. 2011. "Indonesia Military Torture and Kill Indigenous People from West Papua." [https://www.youtube.com/watch?v=JrH9RQWo3p8, accessed May 6, 2013].

Acknowledgments

The author wishes to thank Marcus Mietzner, Richard Chauvel, and Sidney Jones for their reviews, edits, and suggestions. The author also wishes to thank Edward Aspinall for his review and encouragement of this and other works.

Many have contributed to my understanding of Papua within the wider Indonesian context. Many of them may disagree with me: I have learned from them nonetheless. Foremost among those who have contributed to my understanding are colleagues from *Yayasan Sosial Untuk Masyarakat Terpencil* (Yasumat) and the Ob Anggen School, as well as the many Papuans and other Indonesians who are engaged in a painful and often thankless struggle to serve their people. In a land of corruption and surrender, they make the world better, one act at a time, and I have been honored to know them. I also wish to thank: Leila Abu-Gheida, Dewi Arsanti, Michael Bachelard, Javed Bahobol, Jacqui Baker, James Bean, Pria Santri Beringin, Yan Busup, Sigit Darmawanto, George Darroch, Kusno Dermawan, Otniel Elopere, Micah Fisher, Enda Ginting, Salmon Gombo, Jesse Grayman, Scott Guggenheim, Timmi Gurik, Menasye Hilapok, Obeth Holago, Susanne Holste, Calum Hyslop, Alinus Ilitimon, Robert Itlay, Markus Kajoi, the Kalvari clinic, Petra Karetji, Eleanor Kennedy, Murni Kobak, Sonja Litz, Victor Mambor, Brata Manggala, Joerg Meier, Julius Arry Mollet, Timo Mohi, Adrian Morel, Donatus Motte, Adelle Neary, Ita Perwira, Elisabeth Pisani, Jackie Pomeroy, Anissa Lucky Pratiwi, Zakharia Primaditya, Chris Rosado, Tony Ryan, Joseph Pieter 'Odie' Seumahu, Deni Siep, Justin Snyder, Javier Sosa,

Naomi Sosa, Agus Sumule, Andre Therik, Martjin Van Driel, Rode Wanimbo, Oneis Wenda, Pones Wenda, Ted Weohau, Iain Wilson, Jonathan Wilson, Heidi Wisley, Scotty Wisley, Rob Wrobel, Ester Yahuli, and other colleagues who have requested not to be named in Dekai, Jakarta, Jayapura, Manokwari, Sorong, Wamena, and further afield.

Any errors of fact or interpretation are the author's own.

www.ingramcontent.com/pod-product-compliance
Lightning Source LLC
Chambersburg PA
CBHW050552280326
41933CB00011B/1814